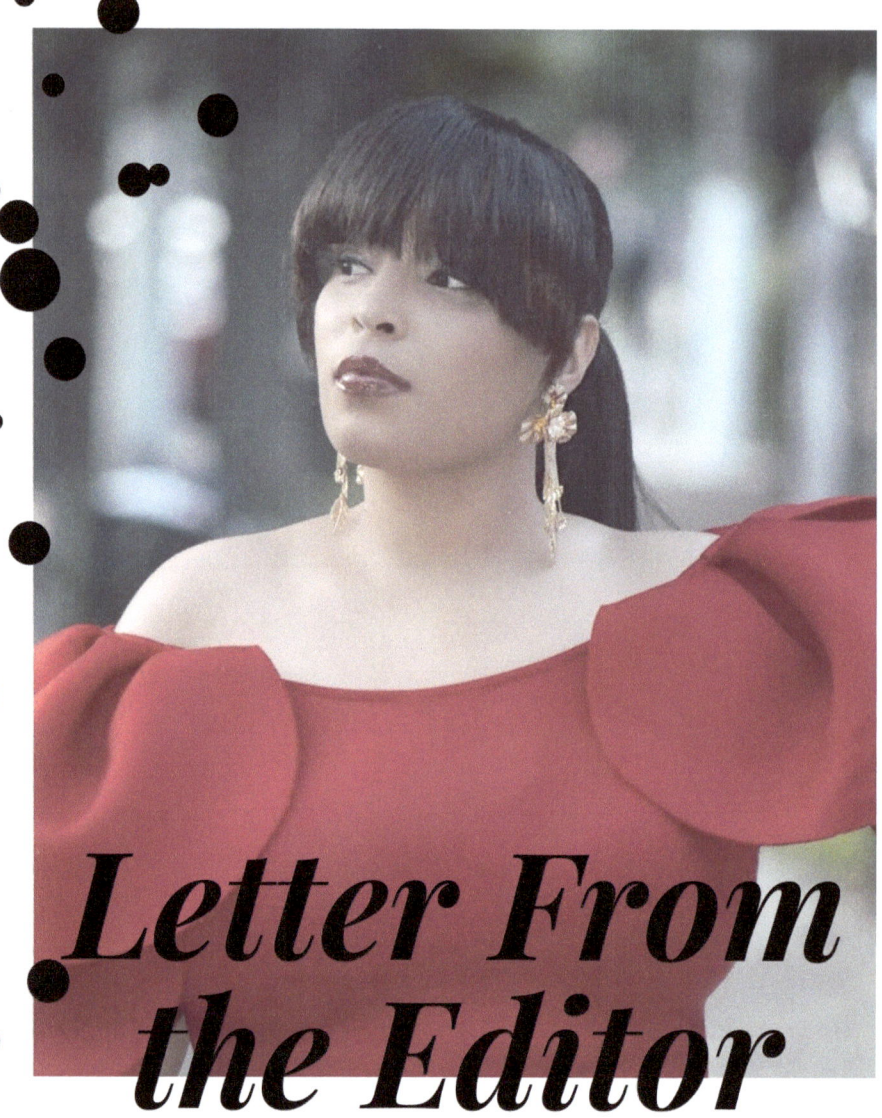

Letter From the Editor

EDITOR-IN-CHIEF PILAR SCRATCH

THIS ISSUE IS ALL ABOUT SPREADING YOUR WINGS AND EXPANSION . WHICH I FEEL IN EVERY CAREER FIELD IS VITAL . WE COVERED THE LOVE & HIP HOP BREAK OUT STAR MARIAH LYNN. SHES A IMMENSELY TALENTED RAPPER FROM JERSEY. MARIAH COMPLETELY HAS SEPARATED HERSELF FROM THE PACK AND IS CREATING A TRANSPARENT PATH ON HER OWN . ITS AWE-INSPIRING . I'M EXCITED FOR THIS SPECIAL EDITION . ENJOY FASHION GXD SQUAD

WWW.FASHIONGXXD.COM

CONTENTS

33 CHEF NA'KIA & CHEF JAY

the dynamic cooking duo. These two amazing chefs are getting the secrets on their success one dish at a time

04 MOGUL LASHES

the national sensation of lashes its starting a empire . Get to know Mogul Lashes CEO

16 SHE BLINKED,LLC

inspiration , love , hope . She Blinked is the amazing healing group that assists women to heal their inner selves

36 TWICE HEADWRAPS

Want a fun festive fashion trend that s easily taking over the nation . Twice head wraps are introducing the casual fashion with couture .

18 MARIAH LYNN - COVER STORY

The Love & Hip Hop NYC Brak out star rises to fame in her next venture . Rising from the ashes Mariah is easily one of the greatest break out stars to hit our air waves and tv screens

08 STYLED BY BREYANNA

Fashion is more than a lifestyle its an epidemic for this young fashionista . Get up close & personal with this personal stylist .

06 DREAMS 2 LIFESTYLE

A Fashion must have that is daring to become a lifestyle . CEO Arshawn gets personal about the secrets to his success .

10 THOMAS THERAPEUTIC

Want to get relaxed ? Want to unearth an amazing skin care brand that assists in curing eczema ? Thomas therapeutic is the key to success.

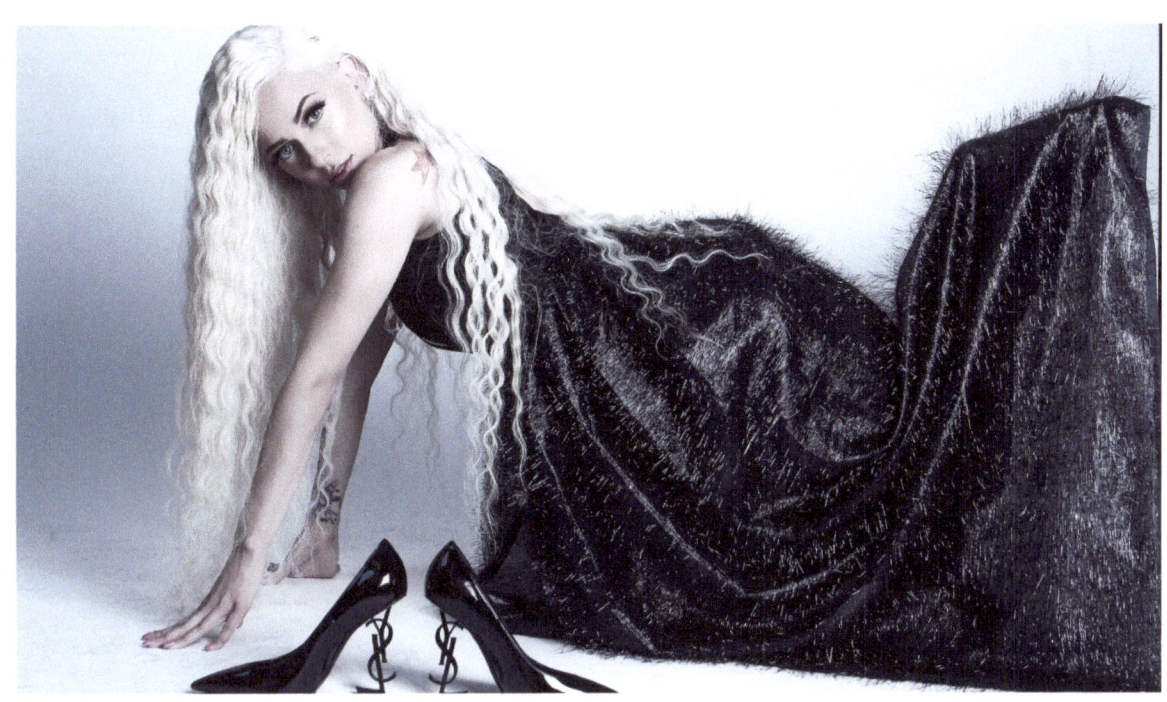

Mogul lashes

By : Lori Day

Mogul Lashes was launched on January 19, 2018 by DyAnn Houston of San Antonio, Texas. The company specializes in cruelty free, luxury mink eyelashes that are handcrafted to perfection and can be tailored to fit any size eye. Mogul lashes are for the everyday woman. A "Mogul" is more than just a wealthy powerhouse; a Mogul is a woman who dreams big, works hard, and strives to reach her goals while empowering others to do the same. When women wear Mogul Lashes, I want them to feel beautiful and to know that they are beautiful! Mogul Lashes are sold exclusively online.

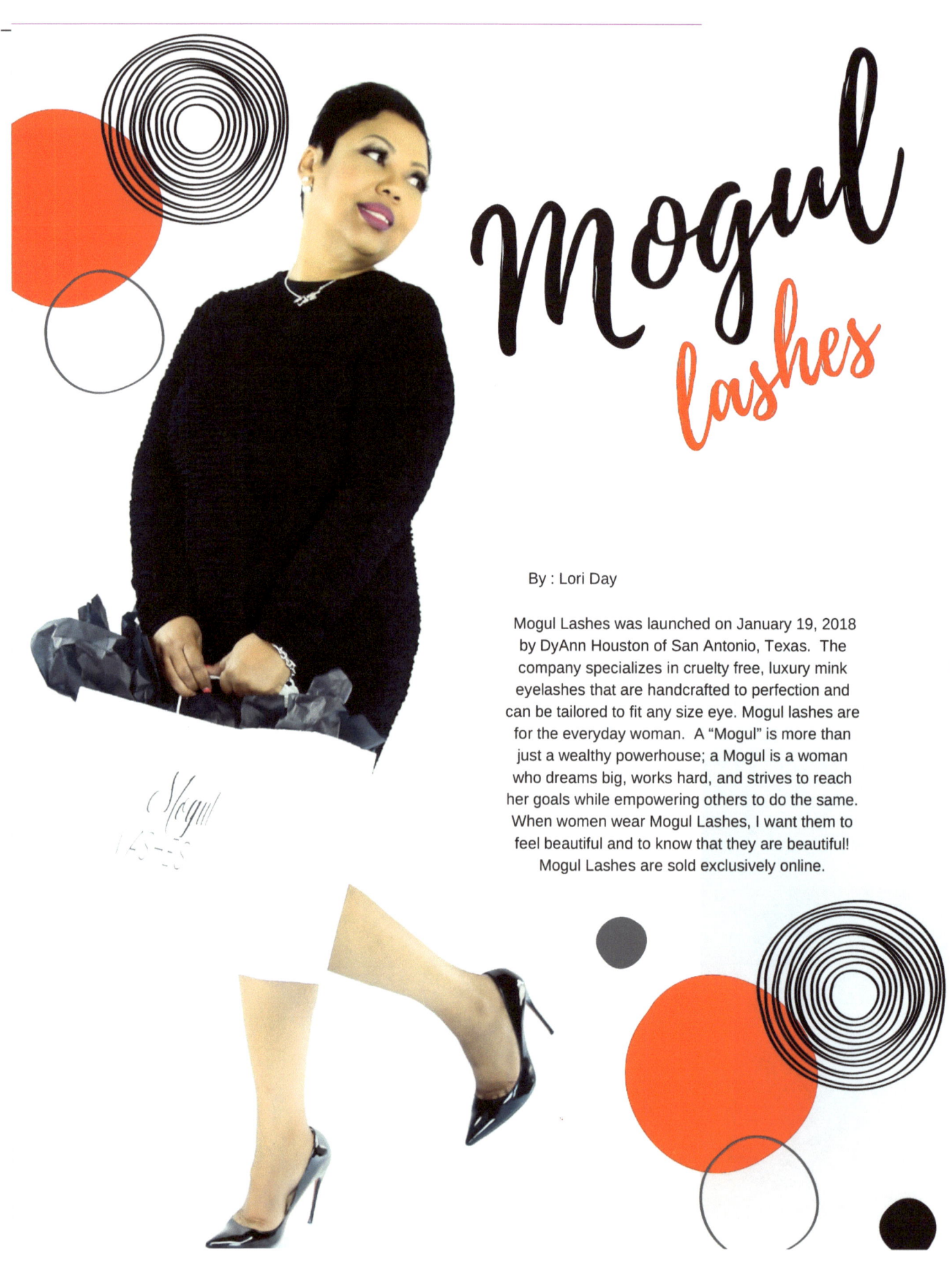

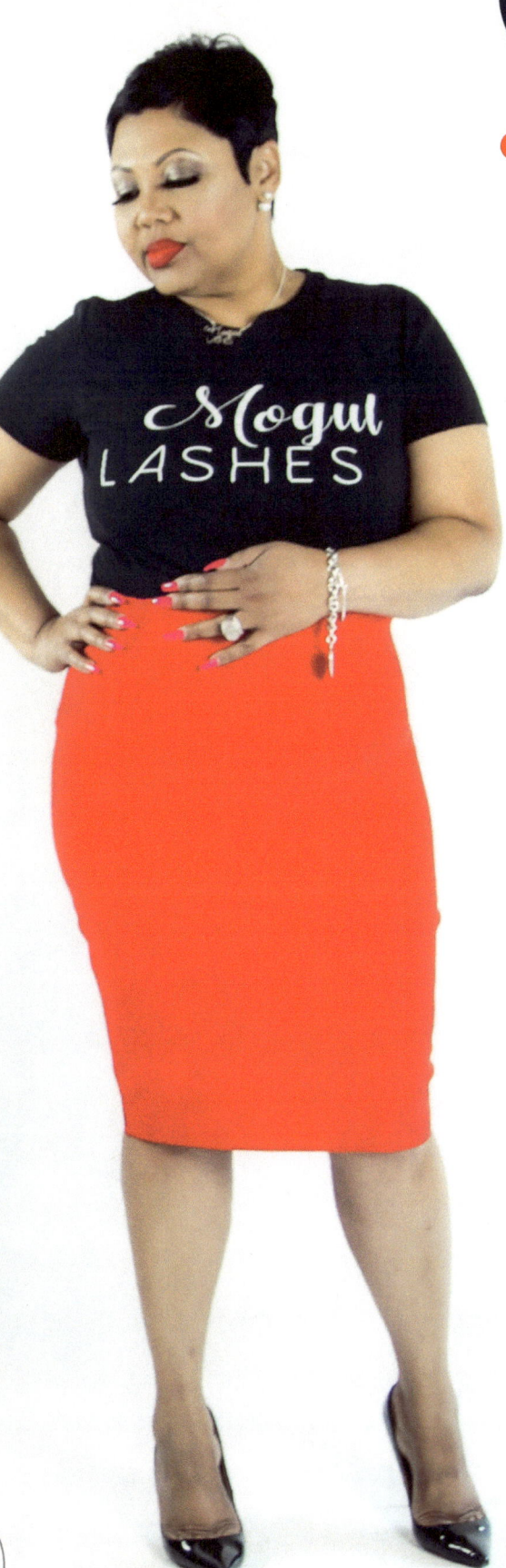

Fashion Gxd Magazine: How did the idea for your business come about?

Dyann Houston (CEO): The idea for Mogul Lashes came about because of my love for lashes and makeup. My desire was to start a cosmetics line after selling makeup for an MLM company. I did a lot of research but still did not know where to start. I took a step back, prayed, and GOD gave me my answer. He told me to start with an eyelash line. I was like "Duh" why hadn't I thought of that before. I am not makeup artist but I am definitely an eyelash connoisseur, so it just made sense.

Fashion Gxd Magazine: How do you find people to bring into your organization that truly care about the organization the way you do?

Dyann Houston (CEO): My business is still in the start-up phase which puts me at an advantage. I can take my time and be selective about choosing the right team. When my business hits the growth phase, I will seek out individuals who possess strong leadership skills, have a heart for others, are approachable, flexible and are not afraid of rejection.

Fashion Gxd Magazine: What three pieces of advice would you give to other people who want to become entrepreneurs?

Dyann Houston (CEO): The first thing I would tell an aspiring entrepreneur is "Dare to Dream!" When you have dreams and aspirations, they are not meant to be sat on. Write them down, do your research, and take time to build your foundation. The foundation is what every structure is built upon and once it has been set in place, it cannot be easily moved. You will need to have the right people around you during this phase so be sure not to share too much too soon and make sure you are sharing with the right people. Sometimes too many opinions can cloud your vision and sometimes diminish it altogether. Remember it is ok to build in silence.

The second thing I would tell someone who desires to start their own business is get a mentor and an accountability partner. A mentor is someone you can connect with that is already in business for themselves. Shadow him or her as much as possible. Ask lots of questions, take their advice, and be open to ideas and criticism. I stated earlier that it is not wise to share everything with everybody, which is why an accountability partner is vital to anyone who in business for themselves. This is a person you can share your goals with, he or she can check on you to make sure you are working towards your goals, you can bounce ideas off of each other, and most of all when you are ready to throw in the towel, he or she can throw it back at you and tell you to keep pushing!

Lastly, and most importantly I would emphasize the need to have good time management and organizational skills. These two are vital to every business regardless of what stage it is in. You must be willing to spend time on your business. I know this can be tricky if you have a full-time job, kids, school, etc. however, you must make time. Begin by carving out 1-2 hours a day and build from there. Invest in a planner to assist with planning out your days, allot time to work on your business, be specific on the tasks you would like to complete, and stick to the plan. This has helped me to not only stay focused, but it has improved my organizational skills because I now know what I am supposed to be doing every day.

Fashion Gxd Magazine: If you had the chance to start your career over again, what would you do differently?

Dyann Houston (CEO): I would have dreamt bigger, sought out a mentor and accountability partner, kept others out of my business and started sooner!

Fashion Gxd Magazine: What would you say are the top three skills needed to be a successful entrepreneur?

Dyann Houston (CEO): To be a successful entrepreneur you must have vision, ambition, and perseverance.

Fashion Gxd Magazine: What have been some of your failures, and what have you learned from them?

Dyann Houston (CEO): There have been lots of failures along the way but I will have to say that one of my biggest failures has been sharing my business ideas with people who do not have the best intentions for me. It is not a good feeling to share something you are passionate or excited about with someone you thought was is in your corner, only to get a negative reaction or derogatory comment. As I stated earlier, I have learned to build in silence and I now know that not everyone is meant to go on my journey with me.

Fashion Gxd Magazine: How do you generate new ideas?

Dyann Houston (CEO): I research my competitors, the industry and the market and then I put myself in my customers' shoes and try to implement things I would want to be offered as a consumer.

Fashion Gxd Magazine: What sacrifices have you had to make to be a successful entrepreneur?

Dyann Houston (CEO): Sacrifice is a strong word because I am doing something I absolutely love. Mogul Lashes is my baby and when you have a baby you reallocate your time to care for your baby. Therefore, I have chosen to utilize my time differently. I have lost a few friends along the way and spent a lot of time and money investing in myself and my business. The return has been worth every second and every cent!

Fashion Gxd Magazine: Where do you see yourself and your business in 10 years? 20 years?

Dyann Houston (CEO): In 10 years I see myself running a successful beauty empire and helping other women to do the same. In 20 years I see myself retired! hahaha

WWW.MOGULLASHES.COM
MOGULLASHES@GMAIL.COM
IG: @MOGULLASHES

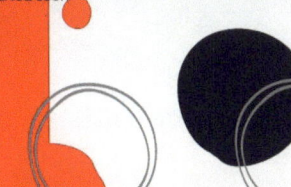

INSTAGRAM: @_DREAMS2LIFESTYLES_
FACEBOOK: DREAMS 2 LIFESTYLES
YOUTUBE: DREAMS 2 LIFESTYLES CLOTHING
WEBSITE: WWW.DREAMS2LIFESTYLES.COM

DREAMS 2 LIFESTYLES

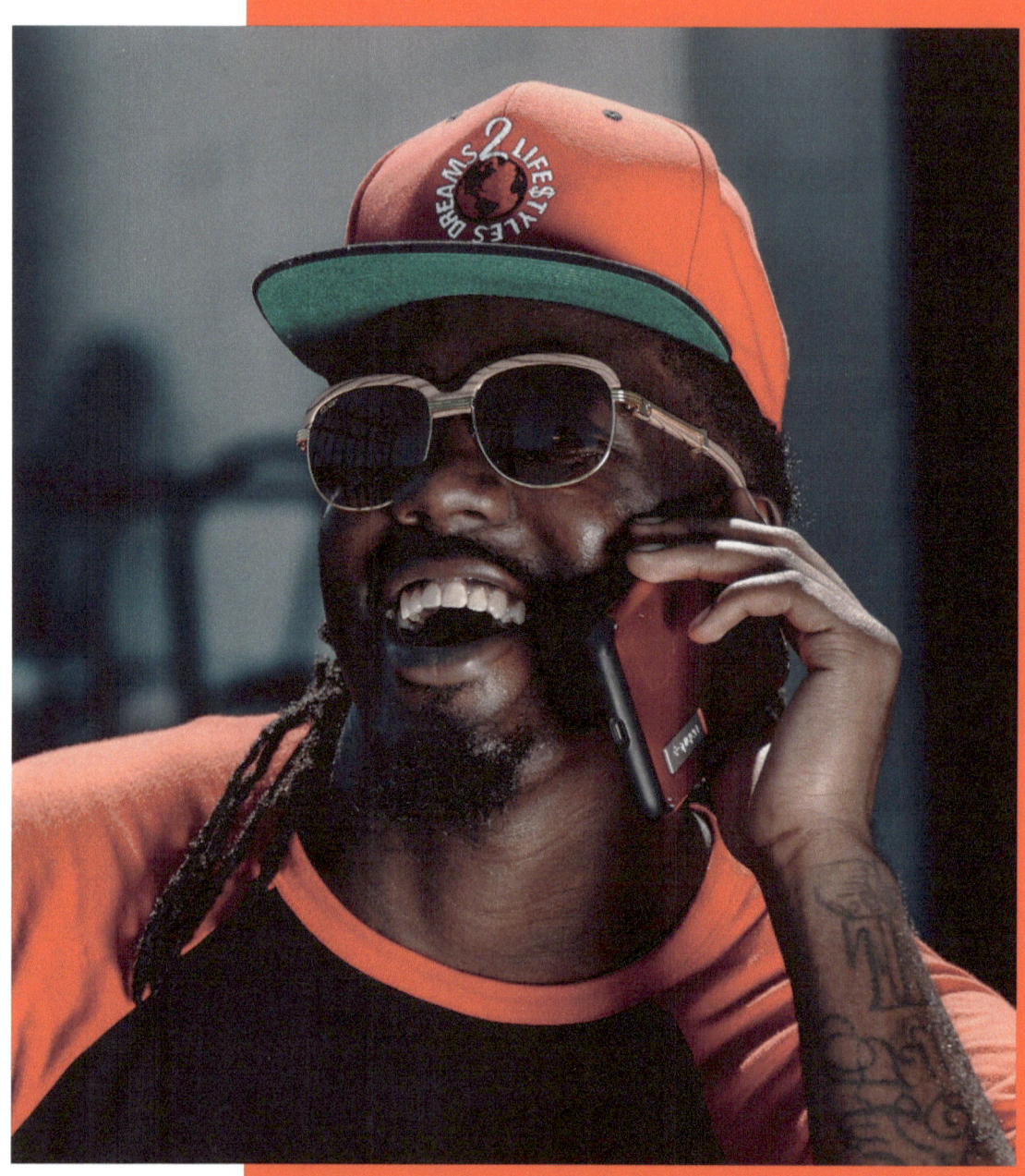

DREAMS 2 LIFESTYLES IS AN AMERICAN INSPIRATIONAL BRAND OF URBAN FASHION. MY VISION WAS TO CREATE A CLOTHING LINE WHERE EVERY PIECE INSPIRE THE POPULOUS TO CHASE THEIR DREAMS. OUR MISSION IS TO LET THE POPULOUS KNOW IF YOU CAN DREAM IT YOU CAN LIVE IT AS WELL. HERE ARE SOME SECRETS TO THE VAST SUCCESS OF THE RISING BRAND

FASHION GXD MAGAZINE

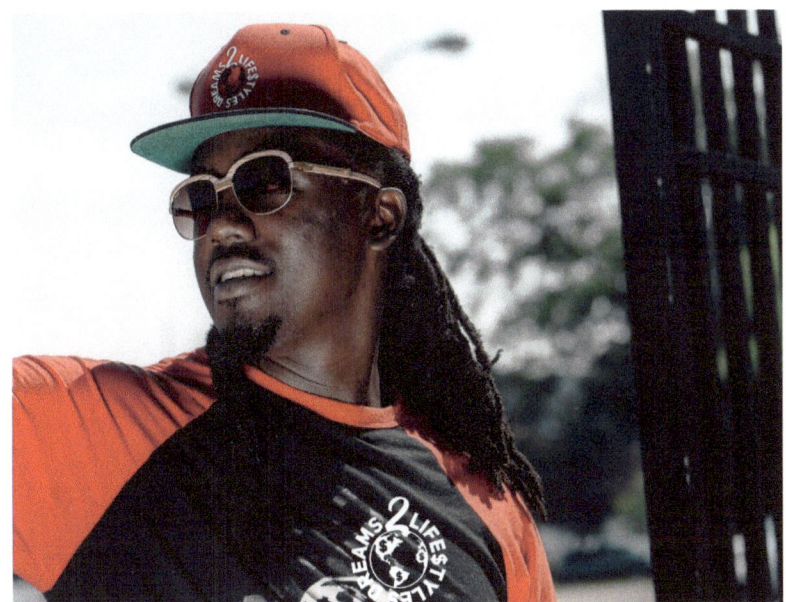
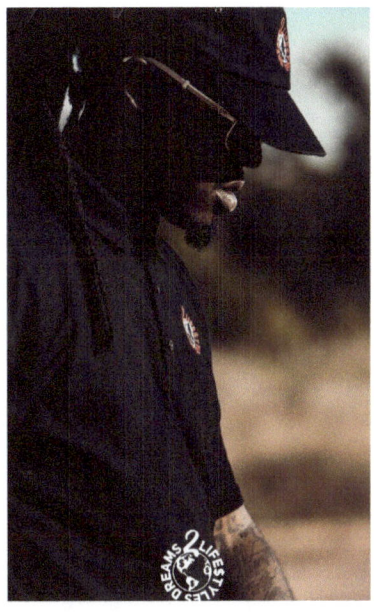

5 TIPS INTO BEING A SUCCESSFUL ENTREPRENEUR

1. Never doubt yourself
2. Master the art of patience
3. Always plan ahead
4. Learn your business from the inside and out
5. Take no days off

5 WAYS I BECAME SUCCESSFUL IN MY FIELD

1. I believed in myself
2. Remain consistent
3. I learn about the industry I'm in from the inside and out
4. I always make sure to be prepared and to plan ahead
5. Keeping a real good work ethic

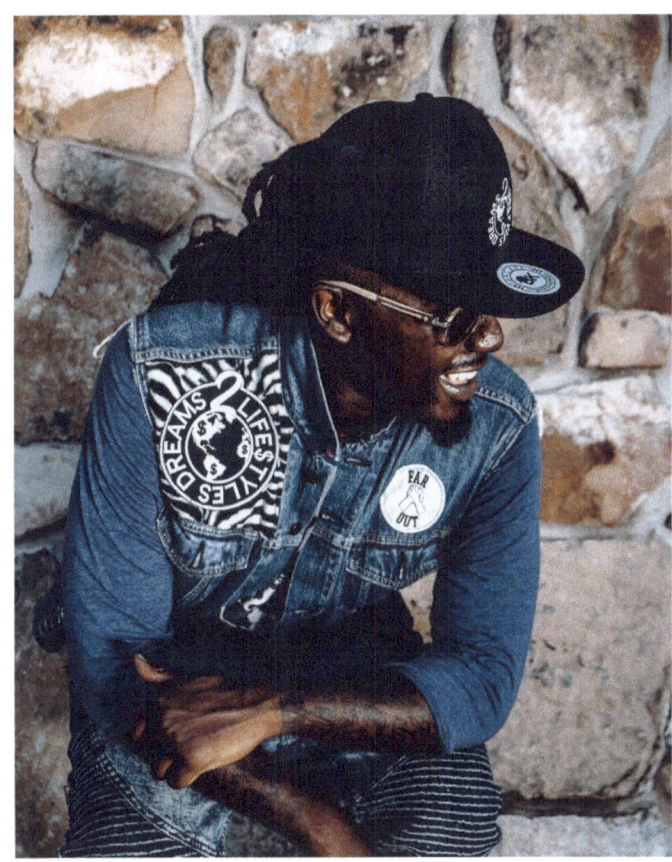

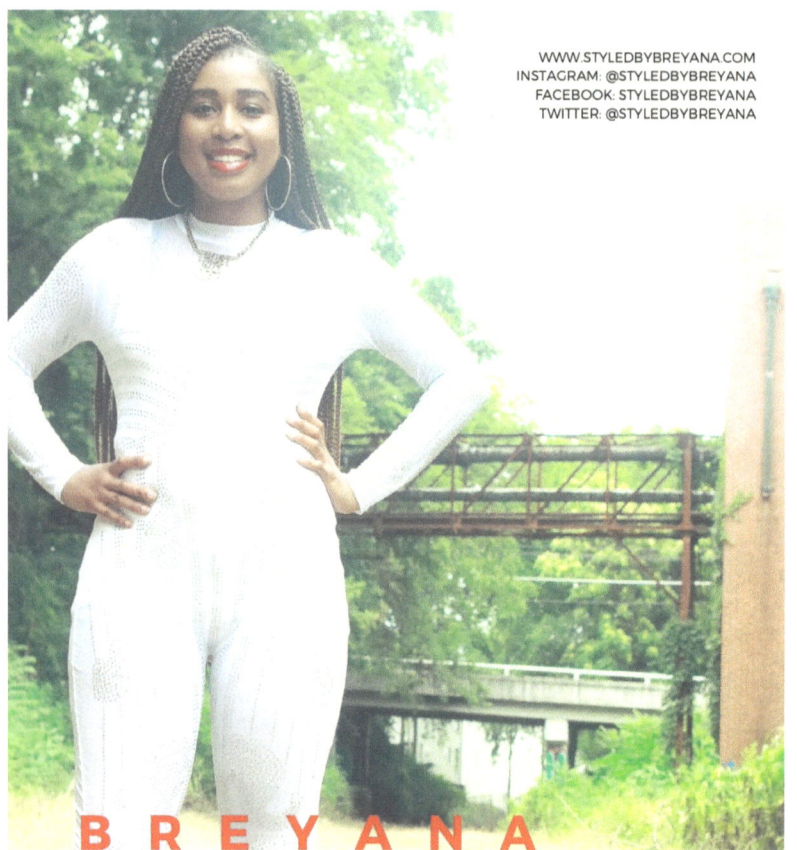

WWW.STYLEDBYBREYANA.COM
INSTAGRAM: @STYLEDBYBREYANA
FACEBOOK: STYLEDBYBREYANA
TWITTER: @STYLEDBYBREYANA

STYLEDBYBREYANA IS AN ONLINE RETAIL AND FASHION STYLING COMPANY DESIGNED TO CATER TO WOMEN (AND MEN) OF ALL SIZES. OUR MISSION/GOAL IS TO CHANGE THE MIND, HEARTS, AND WARDROBE OF MEN AND WOMEN ALL ACROSS THE WORLD BY OFFERING REMOTE AND IN PERSON STYLING SESSIONS AS WELL AS HIGH END FASHION FROM OUR BOUTIQUE..

BREYANA
FASHION'S
NEW IT GIRL

BY FAITH.

On all of my social media outlets (especially on Instagram) I am always telling my followers how God made all of my success possible. A lot of people don't know this, but I never wanted or imagined myself being a business owner. In fact, my brand came from a vision that God had given me. It was the beginning of my first year of college and I had my heart set on being in the medical field (or so I thought!). I was working hard trying to get my GPA as high as possible but I kept hearing a voice urging me to research opening up my own online fashion business. Now, I have always loved fashion but I never seen it as a "real job". Growing up my mom always taught me that college was the way to get a lucrative career and that is all I knew. So with that in mind and the fear of my family's judgement I brushed the thoughts off and kept focusing on my school work. Weeks had passed and the voice had seemed to be getting persistent and eventually I started having dreams and repetitive thoughts about owning my own online store. Eventually I gave in and started researching everything I could about owning my own online business (and surprisingly I started to fall deeper in love the more I learned!). Before you know it by December of 2015 I was ordering merchandise and touching up my website for the store that I was planning on launching in January. I listened to God and asked for guidance throughout the entire process and I made about 5 sales within a week of opening and sold out of one of my first products within a month of being in business.

CONSISTENCY.

Ever since I started my brand, which was in January of 2016, I have always been consistent. I have been consistent with my social media post (I post everyday about three times a day, sharing my products on all of my social media outlets to bring brand awareness to my brand). I want people to see my logo or hear my brands name and say "I've seen/heard that name somewhere before." Even though I am not in the mood sometimes, I redirect my mind to think of the end result which for me is building confidence in women (and men) through styling sessions and allowing them access to fashionable clothing so that they can look the part without the expense. We want to alleviate low self-esteem and promote self-love and empowerment as much as possible.

READING.

The old saying is true reading does expand the mind and vocabulary. I have enjoyed reading books since I was in middle school and I am so thankful that I still enjoy it. I read at least 3-7 articles a day about the fashion industry, business, successful people, sometimes law, and random things that I want to know about (like why is Idris Elba getting married?! That is my husband! Just kidding! Barely!). A lot of people call me "business savvy" and even though I didn't think so at first it is so true. I get a lot of my savviness (if that is a word) and knowledge from reading business articles, books, and listening to Podcast.

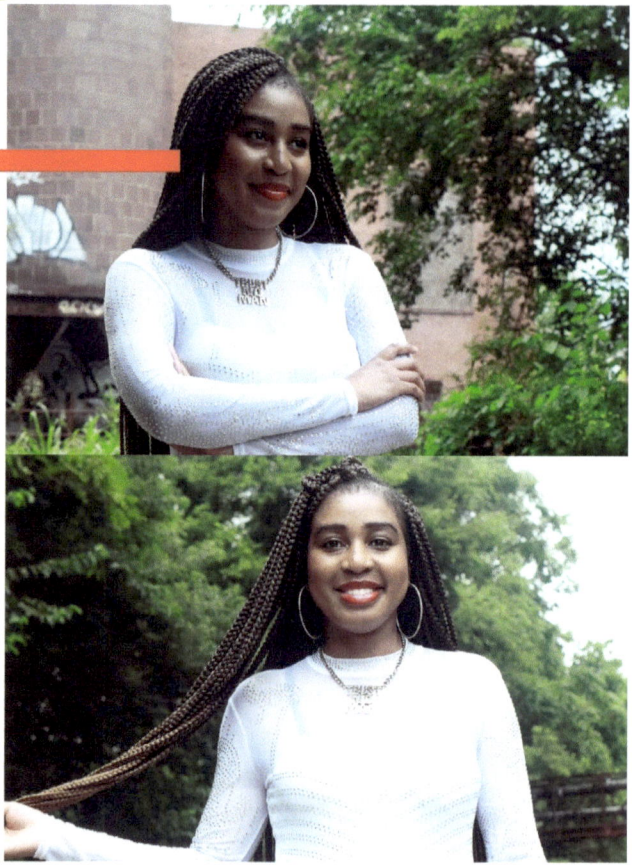

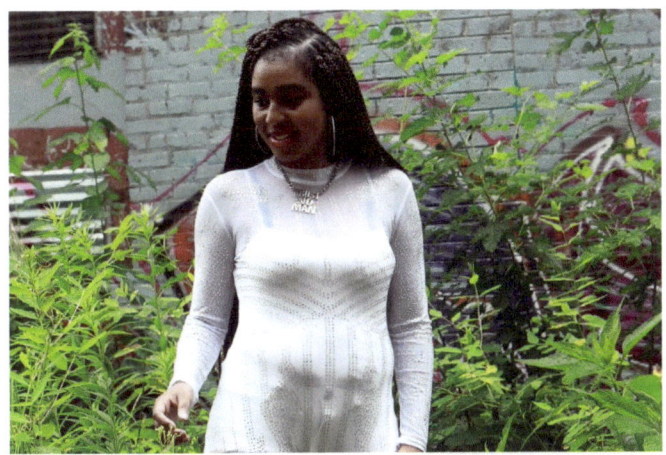

MEET FASHIONS NEW PRINCESS

BEING GENUINE.

As cliché as it may sound being a genuine person has opened up a lot of doors for me. I am the girl that likes to have fun and crack jokes (I display that a lot through my brand especially on my blog and vlogs). I can be extremely outgoing or extremely reserved and I think that mixture is what attracts people to me. I don't try to be someone that I am not and I don't make my brand sound bigger than it is. People can sense authenticity and I believe that is why people enjoy being apart of the Styledbybreyana community—because it is authentic and we are very transparent with everything that we do. The most powerful thing that I have heard so far was someone telling me that they wanted to work with me because "I am so genuine and sweet" that really touched my heart.

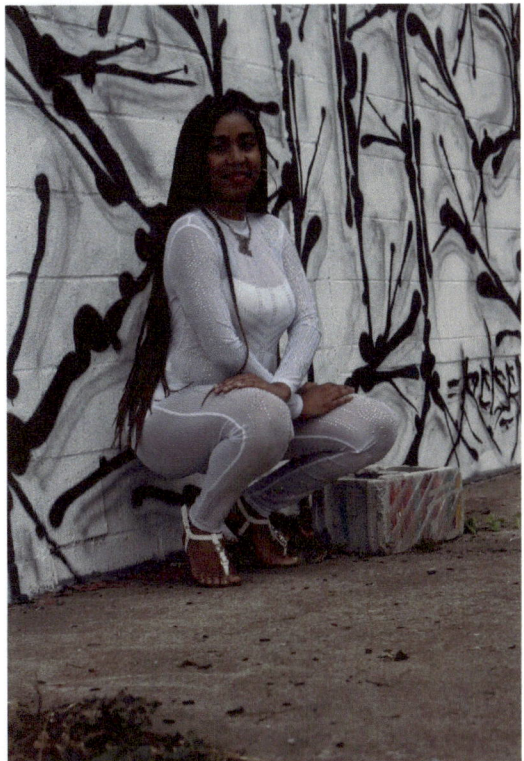

I feel that some people think entrepreneurship is a freedom ticket to not ever having to listen to anyone ever again and in fact, it is the opposite. There are times on this journey of mine where my sales are not as high as the previous month or not as many clients are booking me for a certain season but that has never stopped me. I understand that success doesn't happen overnight and that it might take me 10 years to get my one shining moment but you have to start somewhere.

NEVER GIVING UP.

I use the moments that I am not as busy to perfect my craft and make my brand better and stronger. I always remind myself that if I would have given up I would have never got to style my first celebrity client, I would have never known that people were and are willing to invest in my styling services, and most importantly

INSPIRING OTHERS.

I would have never known that I inspire so many people and that they are actually watching me and cheering me on. I have random people, who I deeply appreciate, sending me messages telling me how much they love what I am doing and giving me words of encouragement. It is an extremely humbling experience.

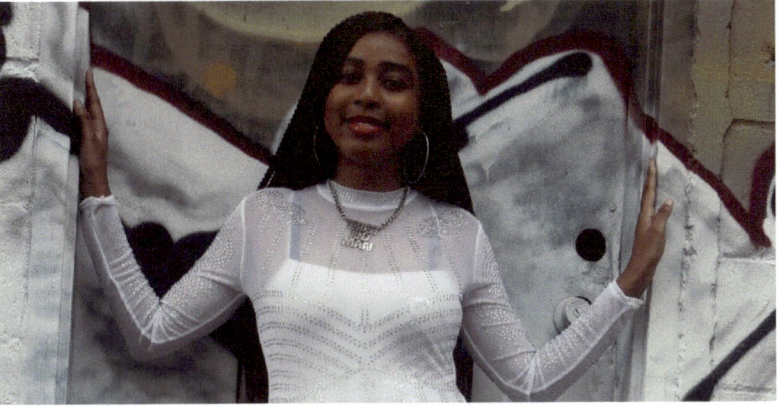

ERIN WHITE

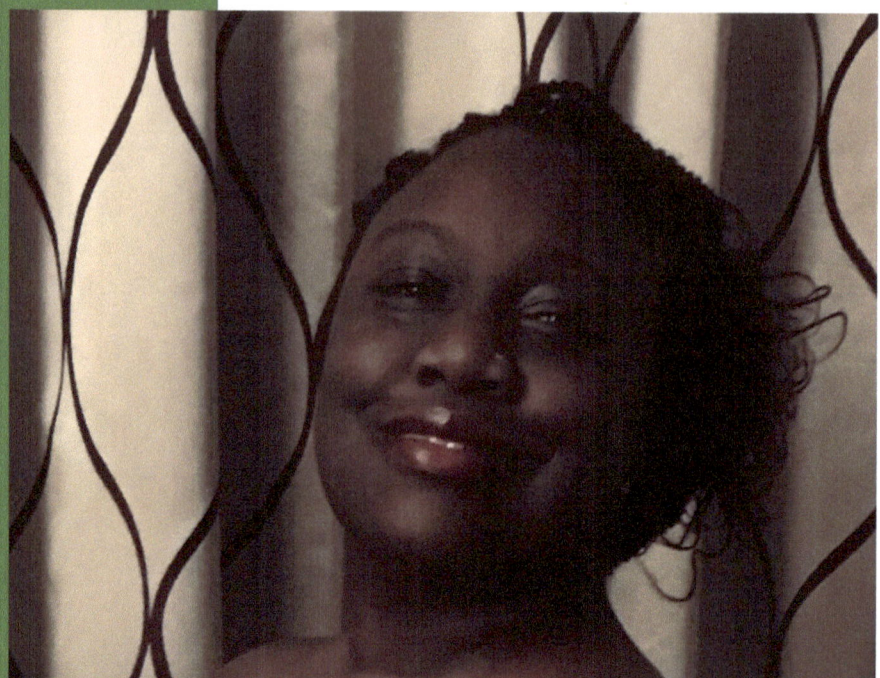

FALL 2018 • ISSUE 17 • VOLUME 7

CEO OF THOMAS THERAPEUTICS

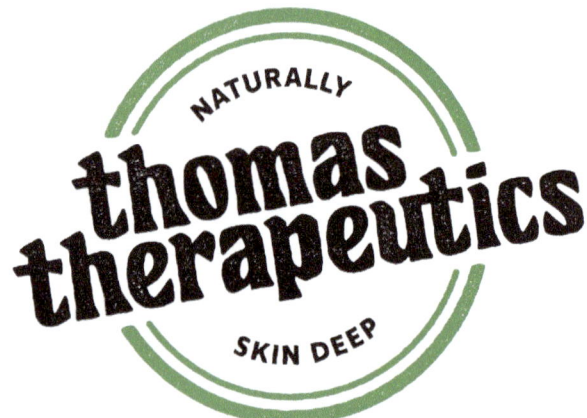

Let's begin with the company name. "Thomas" is the last name of my maternal Grandparents. My mother had me at a young age and her parents raised me, allowing my mother to finish school.

As a child, I suffered from allergies and eczema. I was and am still considering myself allergic to the very air I breathe. I have even developed new allergies within the last two years: pineapple, avocado, and dragonfruit. So, as I find new ingredients, I find myself allergic to them. Thank the Lord for nitrile gloves!!

Anyway, to get back on track...I was raised largely by my maternal Grandmother. Her name was Bobbie June. She recently passed on due to a second battle with cancer. Having survived Breast Cancer and just making ten years cancer-free, she was diagnosed with Stage IV Lung Cancer. During her battle, she took several bouts of radiation and chemotherapy. The chemicals and radiation made her skin so dry and paper thin.

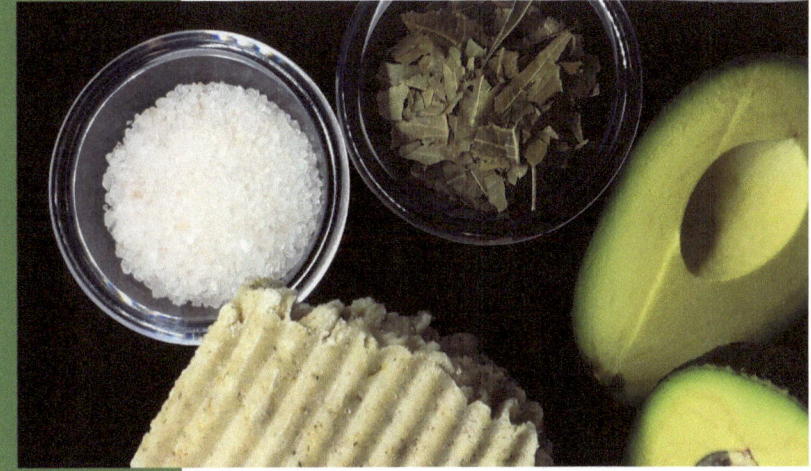

I created a skin regimen for my Grandmother. And though she did not last to see or use it, I have helped others going through the skin issues that come with radiation. And I continue to help by donating a percentage of the profits from the Junebug Skincare Regimen to the American Cancer Society.

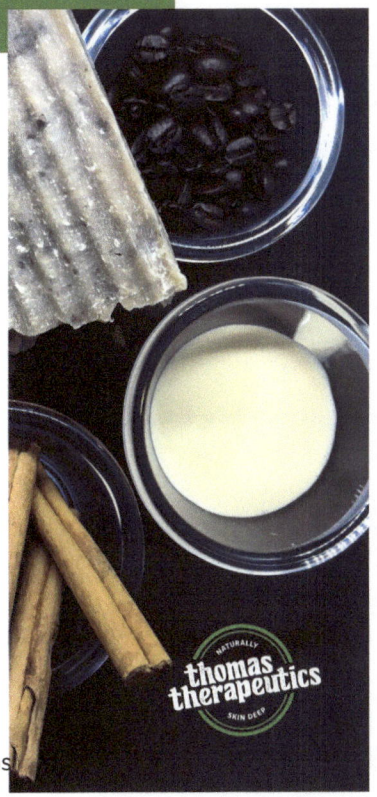

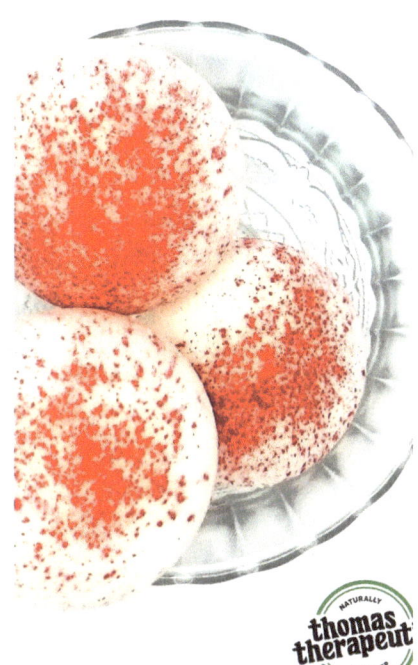

I am an entrepreneur. I make and sell skincare products. My target audience includes those of us with sensitive skin, dry skin, mature skin, and, most of all, delicate skin. I make soaps to treat eczema and psoriasis. I make formulations for Rosacea and Malassezia. As I meet people with different skin conditions, I create products for those exact conditions.

My career as a handmade artisan soap stress began in 2015, well, actually 2011. I just returned home from earning my M. Sc in Biotechnology. My younger sister came out to greet me as I got out of my car at my Grandmother's home. I recognized the plaques, rashes, bumps, and scars.

TIPS FOR CARING FOR YOUR SKIN

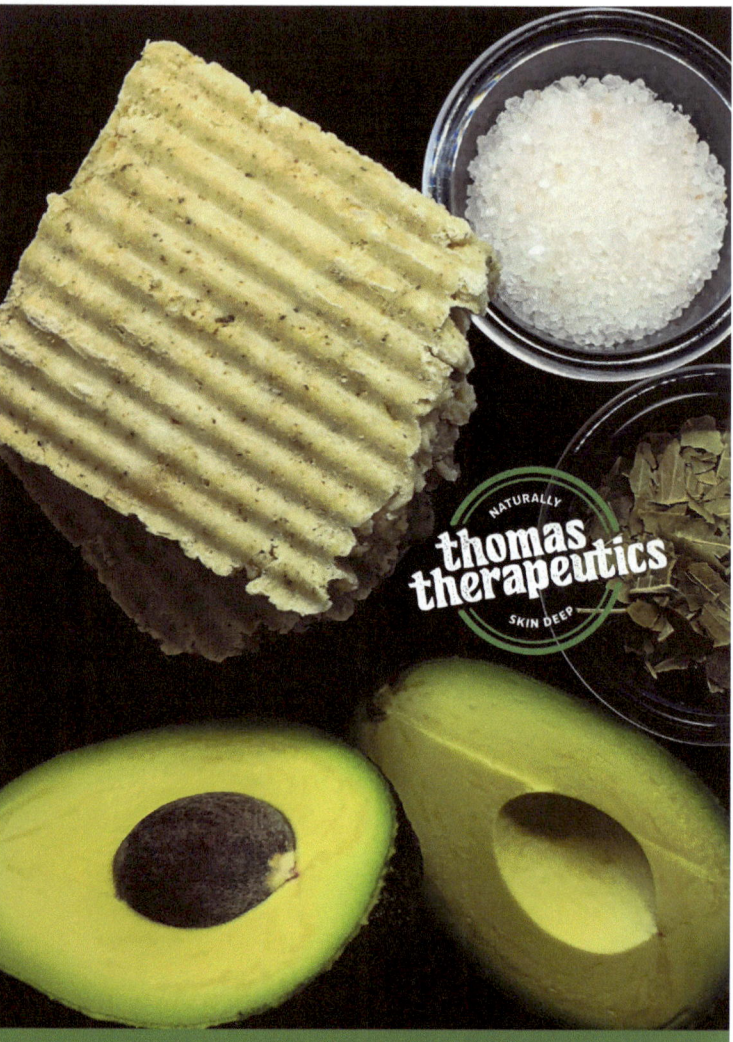

Like me, she has eczema but to a much more harmful degree. At times, her skin has been more eczema than not.

I remember searching the skincare aisles of the grocery stores and Walmart looking for anything that was deemed "eczema-safe" or "safe for dry, sensitive skin" by dermatologists. We tried everything on the market: creams, lotions, salves, combinations of creams, lotions, and salves. Nothing worked long term.

Well, the 20-teens was the beginning of the Shea Butter Movement (as I call it). YouTubers were taking to the internet with their own concoctions and claims of efficacy. I started out by watching these people, most of whom have no Science background.

One day in May of 2014, a friend approached me with the idea to make soap for Mother's Day. I looked at her said incredulously, "What?! Who MAKES soap??? You buy it from the grocery store!!" But she assured me it would be something fun and creative. So, we went to our local art supply store and purchased melt and pour soap bases (something of which I'd never heard). She showed me how to add different scents and pour the molten soap into different molds to make particular shapes.

I did this for awhile mixing in my own ingredients to make soaps for dry or unwell skin. But I wanted to control ALL of the ingredients in my formulations. I wanted to be able to explain each ingredient's purpose to my client's and not be dumbfounded by additives I did not understand.

I began formulating my own concoctions in 2014. I started small and gradually grew from making bars for dry skin to making bars specifically for eczema; from making brightly colored soaps to soaps that brighten the skin. I began to transform my recipe book into a book of scientific data; this ingredient increases these attributes of this added element and this additive reacts negatively with this component.

During my trials and experimentation, I have amassed enormous amounts of information that combined with my B.S. in Microbiology, has empowered me to become an authority on skin conditions. I have products that treat not only eczema but also psoriasis, rosacea, Malassezia, and the list continues. I have been known to concoct formulations for people I have met at vendor events and showcases. If I have not already solved your issue, I will give it my absolute best attempt at creating something that will not only solve your problem but also nurture your skin.

SKINTIPS:

1) I run into people who tell me that their skin routine consists of wiping their faces with a warm, wet washcloth. There needs to be a cleansing step in your skincare routine...even if it only happens once per day.
2) Coconut oil does not solve everything for everyone. Yes, it is possible to use the oil cleansing method. Some do so using coconut oil but this method is very specific to skin type. Please thoroughly research your cleansing method before committing to it.
3) African Black soap is not a cure-all. Yes, again, this product works for some, but it can be extremely drying for others. Using products on your skin that are ultra-drying can cause your skin to overproduce oils. So, you are actually causing your skin to become more oily and more acne-prone. Again, thoroughly research any cleansing methods before applying them to your skin.

Septemberr 2019 / Issue 18

LO
OK

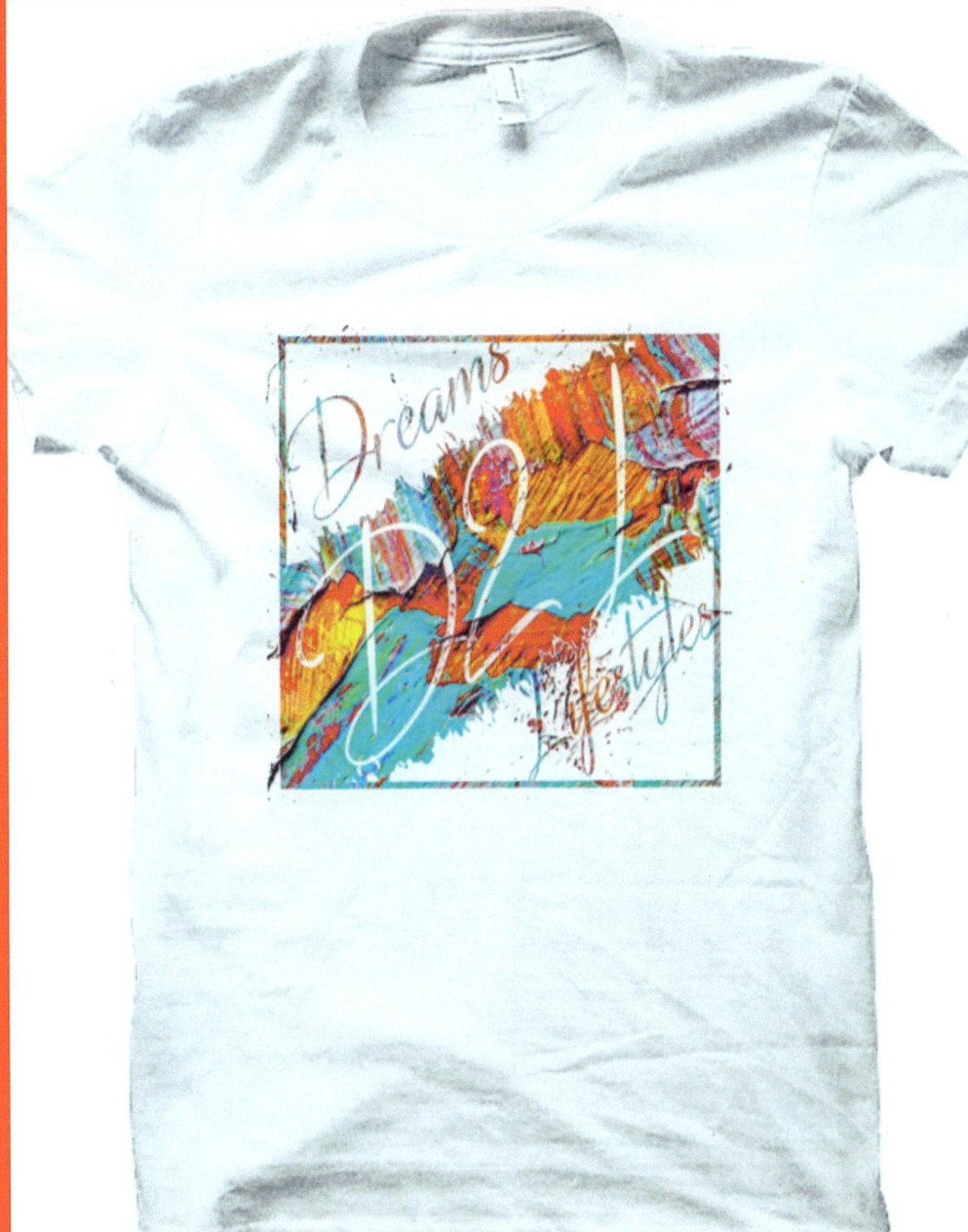

01
PROMOTIONAL CODE
Use Promo code: Dreams 2 Lifestyles for a 15% discount on our special edition Dreams 2 Lifestyles Signature Tee

02
SOCIAL MEDIA HANDLES
INSTAGRAM: @DREAMS2LIFESTYLES
FACEBOOK: DREAMS 2 LIFESTYLES
YOUTUBE: DREAMS 2 LIFESTYLES CLOTHING
WEBSITE: WWW.DREAMS2LIFESTYLES.COM

AMBITIOUS CHIC

BE BOLD! BE FIERCE! BE YOU!

By John Yuki

Ambitious Chic is a brand that sells shoes, clothing, and accessories for an affordable price. Take a look at the exclusive interview with the rising new brand.

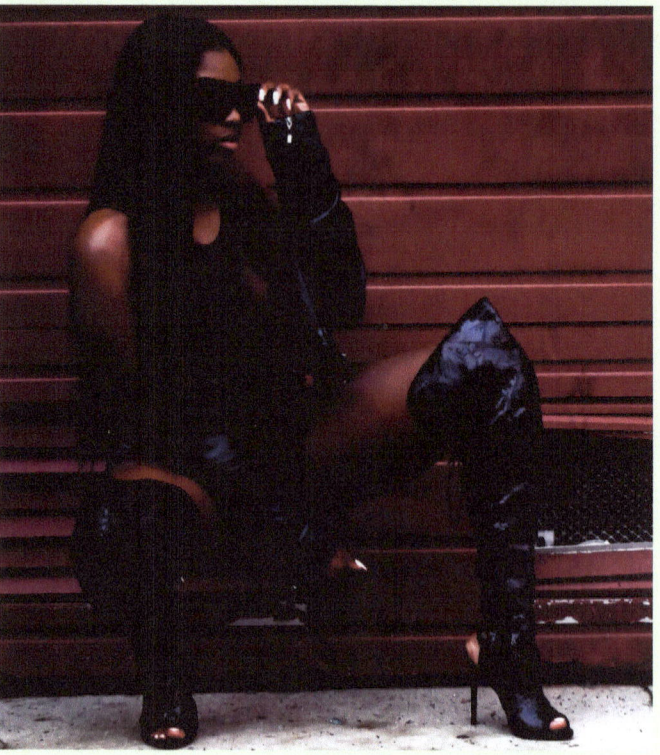

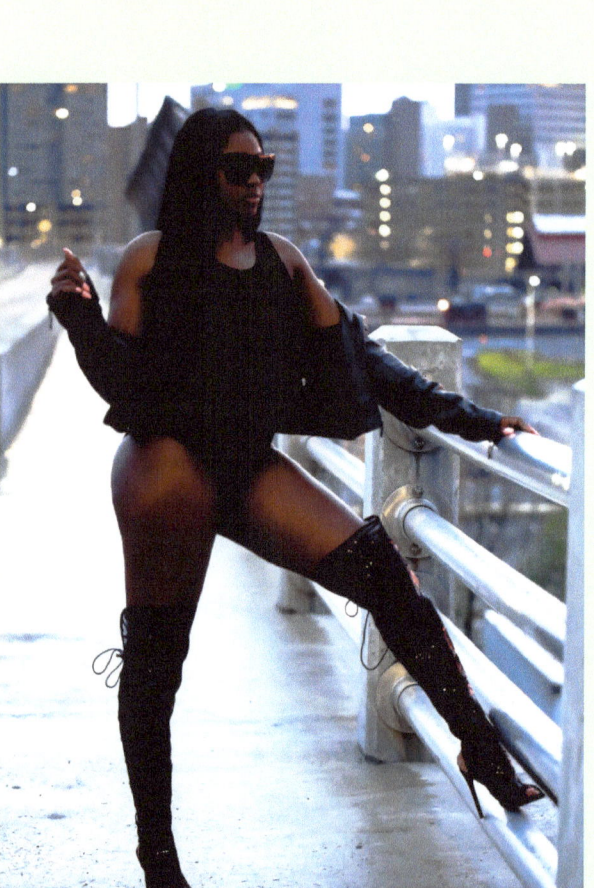

Fashion Gxd Magazine : How did the idea for your business come about?

AMBITIOUS CHIC: Well to start off, I love fashion!! I love cute shoes, dresses, accessories, all of that stuff. I brought the idea of starting a shoe and clothing line so that I can make it affordable for people who cannot afford fashionable good quality products.

Fashion Gxd Magazine : How do you find people to bring into your organization that truly care about the organization the way you do?

AMBITIOUS CHIC: As of right now, I have not had the opportunity to find people to bring into my organization. But, when I do have the opportunity to find people and bring them into my organization, I will make sure all their qualities match up to what my organization stands for.

Fashion Gxd Magazine : What three pieces of advice would you give to other children who want to become entrepreneurs?
AMBITIOUS CHIC: Three pieces of advice I would give to children who want to become entrepreneurs I would say Find your Passion, Embrace your Difficulties, and Network everywhere you go

Fashion Gxd Magazine :If you had the chance to start your career over again, what would you do differently?
AMBITIOUS CHIC: I would wanna find someone to invest into my company so that they can help bring my brand alive.

Fashion Gxd Magazine :What would you say are the top three skills needed to be a successful entrepreneur ?

AMBITIOUS CHIC: The top three skills to become a successful entrepreneur in my opinion would be to always have Persistence, Work Ethic, and be Open Minded and work hard!

Fashion Gxd Magazine :What have been some of your failures, and what have you learned from them?

AMBITIOUS CHIC: Some of my failures are just constantly buying lots of products and not making enough sales.I feel as though it's hard to find customers to bring to my online website. But by me vending at different events I do good on sales.

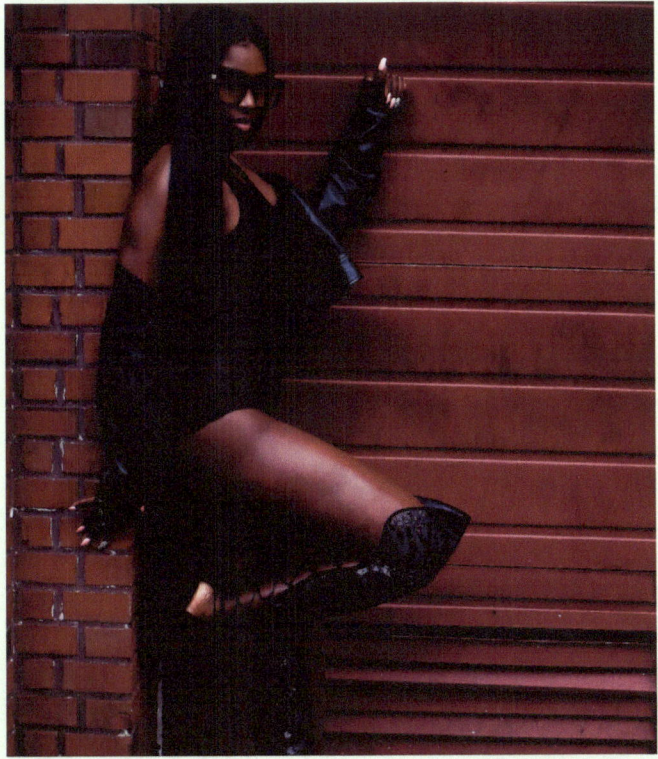

"NETWORK EVERYWHERE YOU GO"

OFFICIAL WEBSITE: WWW.AMBITIOUSCHICS.COM
OFFICIAL SOCIAL MEDIA:
FACEBOOK.COM/AMBITIOUSCHICS
.INSTAGRAM.COM/AMBITIOUS_CHICS
TWITTER: @AMBITIOUSCHICS

By Stephanie Chan

Fashion Gxd Magazine : How many hours do you work a day on average?

AMBITIOUS CHIC: I usually work 12 hours a day.

Fashion Gxd Magazine :Describe/outline your typical day?

AMBITIOUS CHIC: I work Full-time/part-time. I cater to my kids everyday, I check out what's trending on social media, to see how I can get my brand involved.

Fashion Gxd Magazine : How has being an entrepreneur affected your family life?

AMBITIOUS CHIC: Being an Entrepreneur has affected my family life in a good way, because my children have been helping me along the way to create my successful business.

Fashion Gxd Magazine :What motivates you?

AMBITIOUS CHIC: My children help motivate me honestly, they are creative just like me and they help provide me with great ideas, I call them my team because they help or at least try to help me with my business as much as they can.

Fashion Gxd Magazine: How do you generate new ideas?

AMBITIOUS CHIC: I generate new ideas by being different, and Inspired by my Creativity!

Fashion Gxd Magazine : What sacrifices have you had to make to be a successful entrepreneur?

AMBITIOUS CHIC: The sacrifices I had to make to become a successful entrepreneur would be spending a lot of money on things I really shouldn't have, because I realized later that there was a different route I could have taken to become a successful entrepreneur, even though I do not think I am a successful entrepreneur I am very close to becoming one.

Fashion Gxd Magazine : Where you see yourself and your business in 10 years? 20 years?

AMBITIOUS CHIC: In 10 years I see my business "AMBITIOUS CHIC " having at least 5 store locations in high volume cities, having more inventory on my website, hoping I have a better mindset. In 20 years I see my business having over 100 store locations, collabing with other businesses, starting a foundation, and making more great moves!

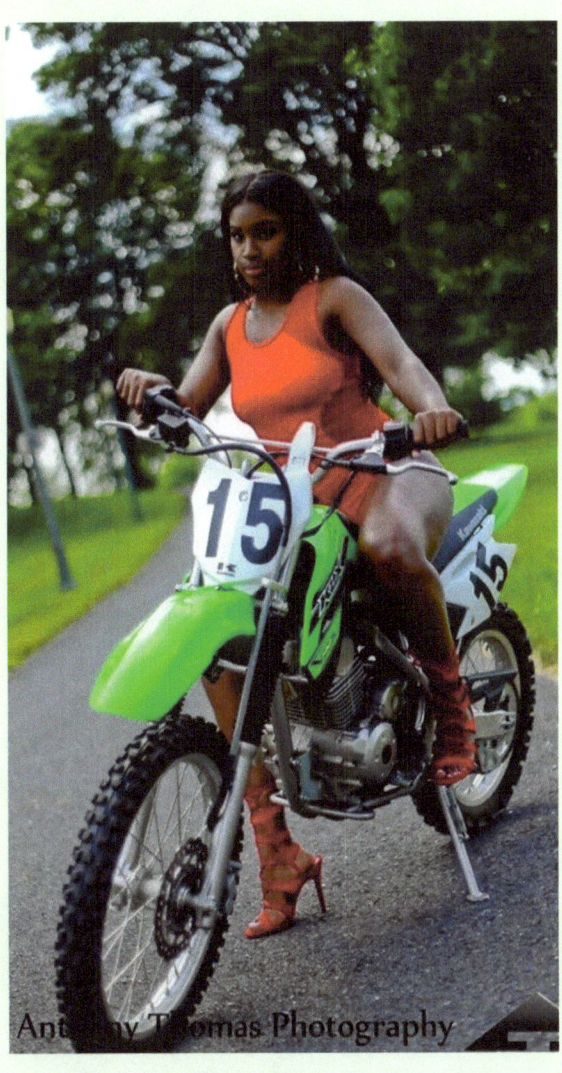

Anthony Thomas Photography

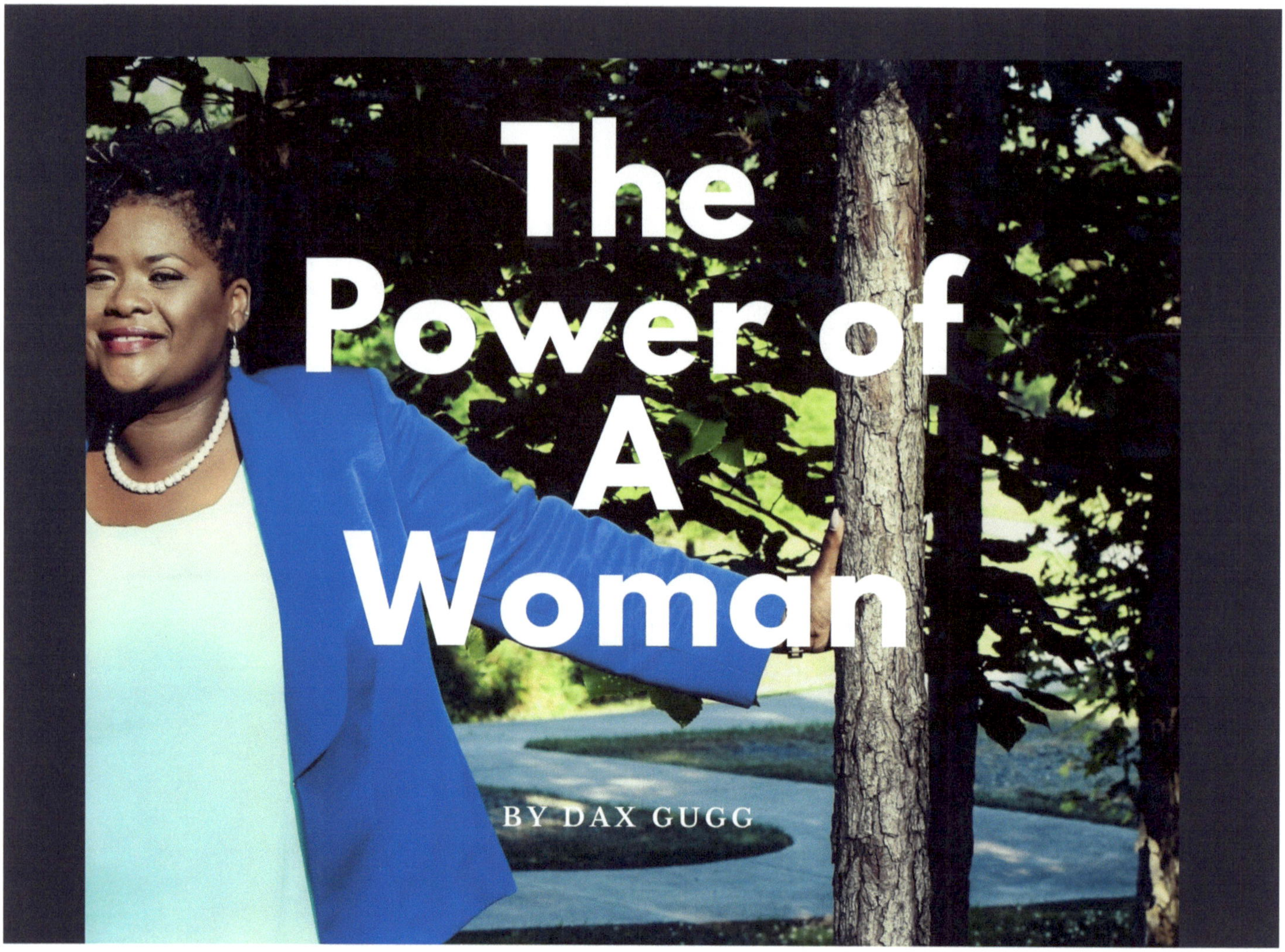

The Power of A Woman

BY DAX GUGG

SheBlinked LLC is a public speaking company that helps organizations and individuals in the area of personal and professional growth, by bridging the human/business connection. We believe that one must overcome personal fears to be successful professionally. We specialize in many areas of leadership transformation touching on soft people skills, commumication, conflict resolution, customer service, and social responsibility.

After spending over 26 years in retail, I saw an alarming trend in leadership gaps. I have seen many talented individuals leave an organization due to poor leadership styles and personal conflict. It is challenging balancing work and life while attempting to lead others. My goal was to impact people beyond the paycheck thus improving associate/customer relations while driving business results. Which led me to actively development.

mentor well over 200 individuals at different levels of leadership. I have served as a moderator for multiple leadership conferences, as well as event chairperson and later event host.

Our ideal customers would be organizations or individuals that seek practical tools to enhance their personal and professional growth in the area of transformational leadership. Those struggling to connect with employees or business partners in the areas of soft people skills, conflict resolution, connecting with customers and professional

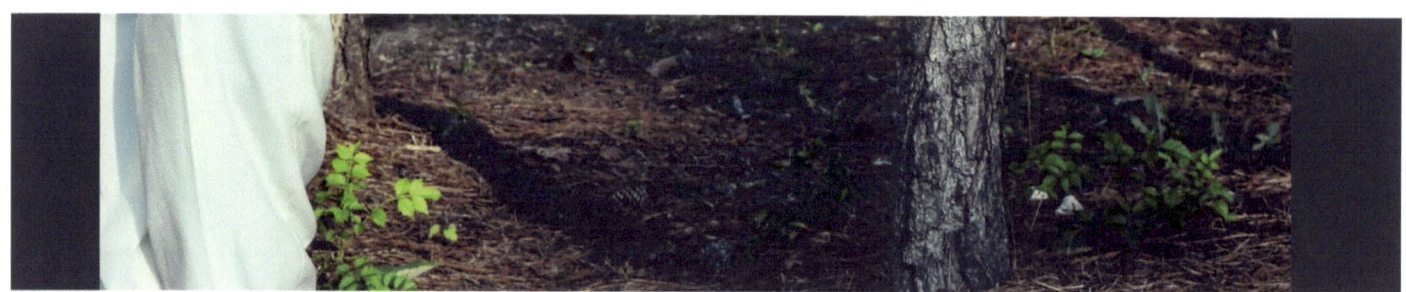

SheBlinked, LLC

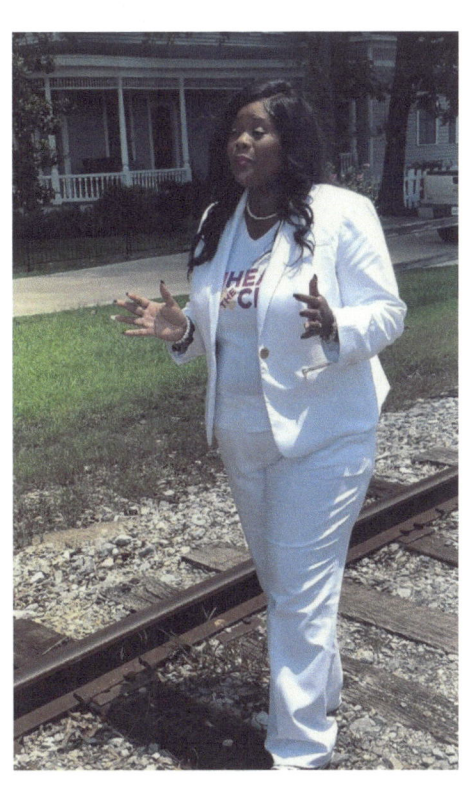

We at SheBlinked LLC believe that is our social responsibility to give back. I will tell you that I have been afforded many opportunities to do so. That's why I founded Heal The City Incorporated, a not-for-profit public speak organization that brings together a dynamic group of leaders that share my passion for sowing back into the community.

We tackle tough issues such as mental health issues, molestation, domestic violence, suicide, rape, low self worth, relationship and leadership issues.

I believe wholeheartedly that we are more alike than we are different. I also believe that if we are to ever excel professionally, it is imperative that we deal with the junk that holds us hostage personally.

Laurinda Andujar
CEO/Owner

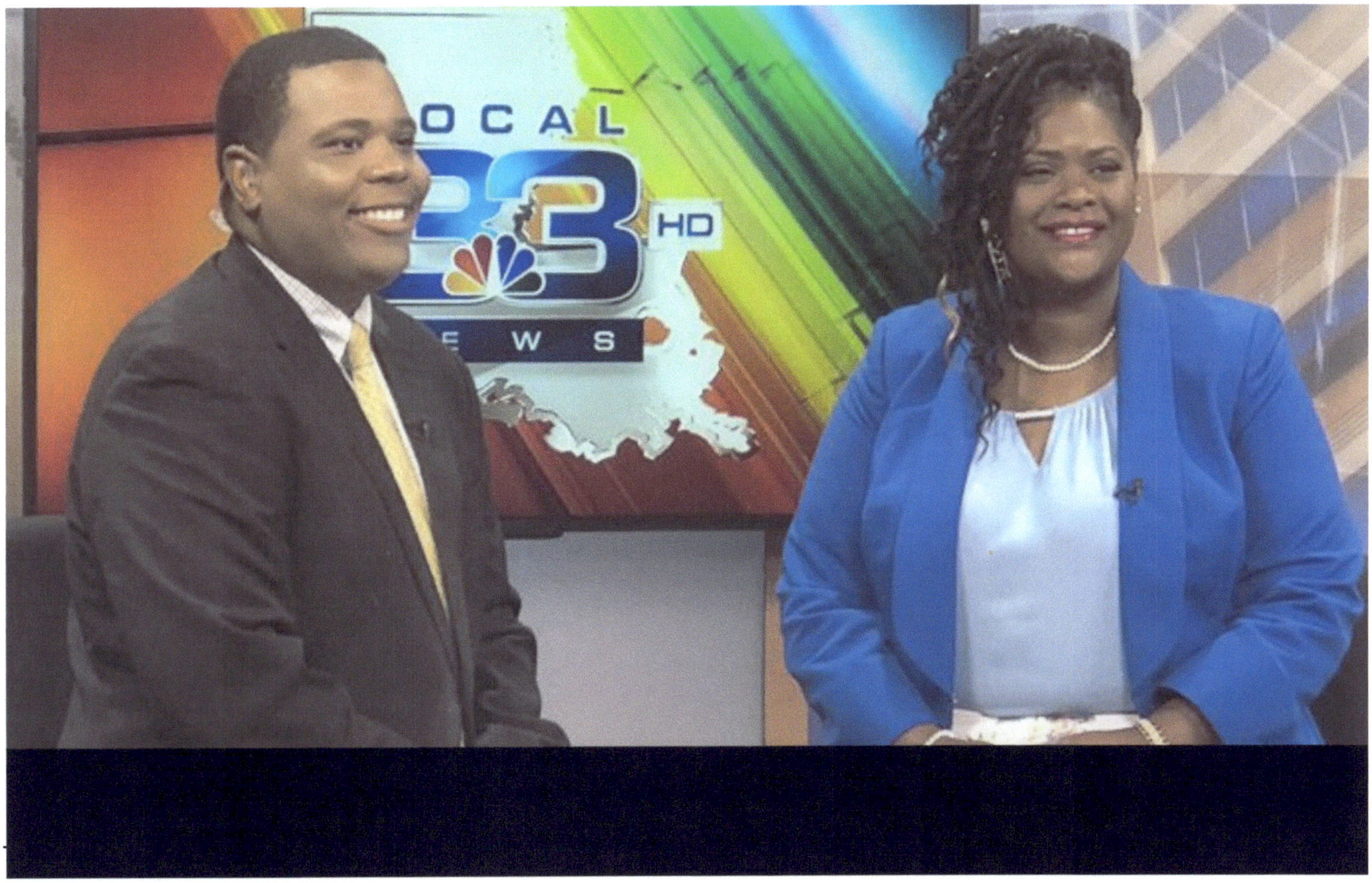

COVER STORY

MARIAH LYNN

THE HIP HOP GODDESS

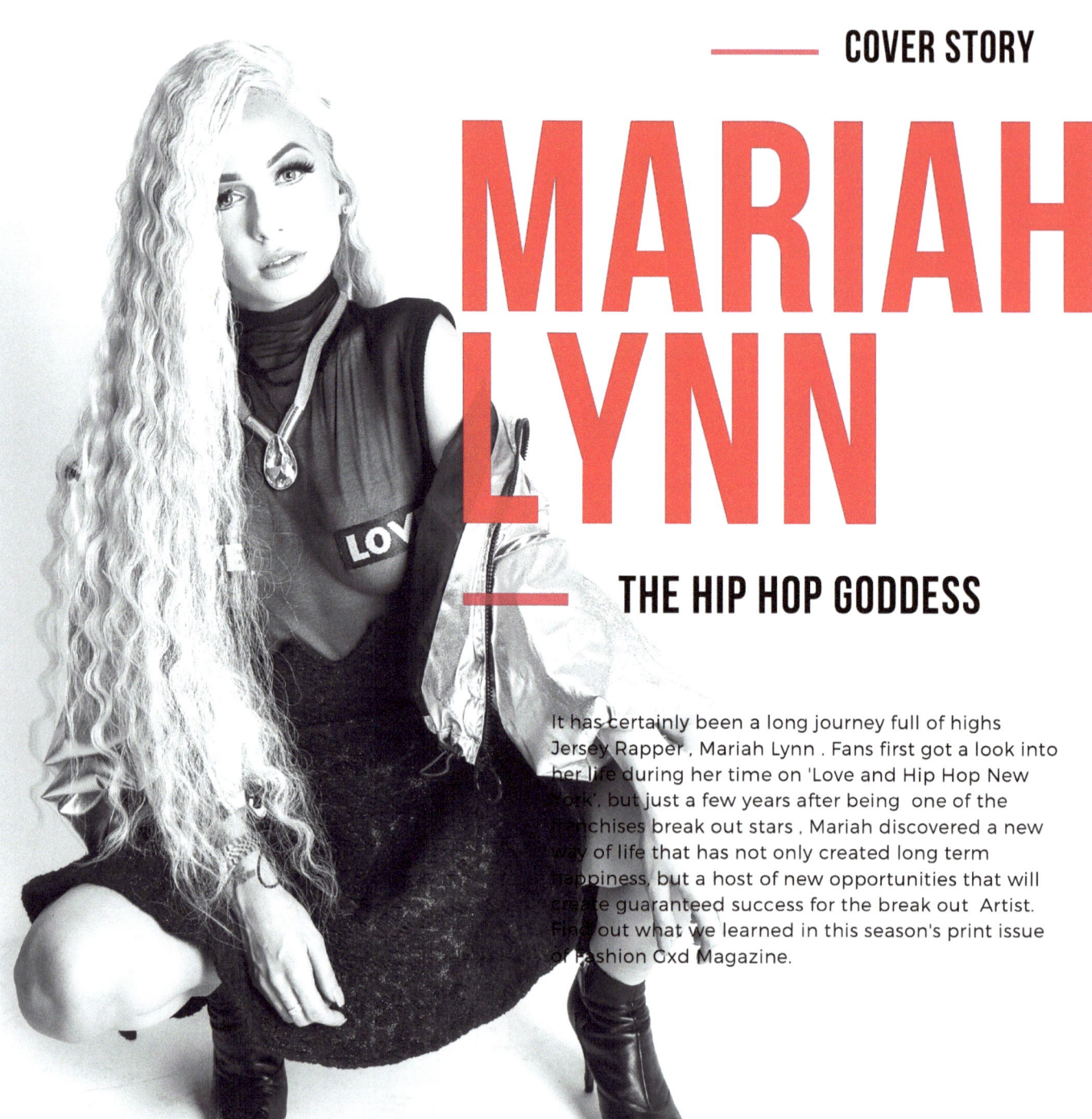

It has certainly been a long journey full of highs Jersey Rapper, Mariah Lynn. Fans first got a look into her life during her time on 'Love and Hip Hop New York', but just a few years after being one of the franchises break out stars, Mariah discovered a new way of life that has not only created long term happiness, but a host of new opportunities that will create guaranteed success for the break out Artist. Find out what we learned in this season's print issue of Fashion Gxd Magazine.

MAKEUP: @FACESBYNYDIA
ASSIST. MUA: @KELLYCORTLAND_MUA
PHOTOS: @NOTORIOUSPHOTOS, @MOMENTSBYMELLO
DESIGNERS: @SHAQUANNA_THEDESIGNER
@MARQUISEFOSTER , @OG_KREE
LEAD WARDROBE STYLIST : @ANDREVONBOOZIER
ASSISTANT STYLIST : @BEAUTYBYDEFAULT
ACCESSORIES: @VELZMONROE , STUDIO:

Written by SICARAH
Photos by NOTORIOUS PHOTOS

"WHAT'S THE 411?"

THE NEW FACE OF HIP HOP

Written by SICARAH
MAKEUP: @FACESBYNYDIA
ASSIST. MUA: @KELLYCORTLAND_MUA
PHOTOS: @NOTORIOUSPHOTOS,
@MOMENTSBYMELLO
DESIGNERS: @SHAQUANNA_THEDESIGNER
@MARQUISEFOSTER , @OG_KREE
LEAD WARDROBE STYLIST :
@ANDREVONBOOZIER
ASSISTANT STYLIST : @BEAUTYBYDEFAULT
ACCESSORIES: @VELZMONROE , STUDIO:

Sicarah: Hey what's up it's your girl Sicarah and right now I'm with rapper Mariah Lynn.
First I want to say congratulations on being on the Fashion Gxd Magazine cover.
Also, your tab reloaded single featuring Remy Ma is bomb by the way.

Mariah Lynn: Thank you so much !

Sicarah: You're welcome. So with your music such as "Tab Reloaded"and "Once Upon A Time" you're very confident. As well , you have a lot of ambition and you show people you can get anywhere you want to be....

Mariah Lynn: Absolutely....

Sicarah: What advice would you give to women ? As far as you know basically reaching their dreams and getting to where you are today?

Mariah Lynn: Stay true to yourself ! I know that it's hard as a female to be out there and not get lost in the sauce . Losing your morals and you know "bow down" in certain situations. I promise you that if you feel like you have to you know do something that compromises your morality or you know just your respect for yourself as a woman don't do it ! I've been in many situations I could have been further than where I am if I had done things that I didn't necessarily want to do. I didn't end up doing those things. You know! I'm still here still fighting. I just want to let the women out there know that in a male dominated industry we're starting to dominate.

Sicarah: Yes! You can say that again. I'm so excited women empowerment all day every day!

Mariah Lynn: Indubitably....

Sicarah: Also, on the show like you said; there's certain things that show you don't know.You don't really know what's going on all the time. What is one thing you would want your viewers to know about you that they may not know?

Mariah Lynn: Yeah, I mean again if I return this year you guys will see a little bit more into my personal life. You will see me taking care of my sisters, and my siblings. My mother is fighting her addiction and everything. It's extremely hard for me sometimes. Overall, you have to push through; no matter what. When women empower other women it makes a lot of things cohesive for everybody. Especially, like you can't kick somebody when they're down. That's what I tend to not do. I just try to empower an uplift. You know promote positivity and stuff. Whereas on the show I'm pretty much villainized. On the show its shows a lot of my reaction and not enough of the provoking.

Sicarah: Yes you're very influential. What are three people who Influenced you? doesn't have to be music , overall inspirational people?

Mariah Lynn: Terrell Everett, Victoria Ramos, Iceland Gail, Daniel, Damian , Elias, my sisters, my brothers, my best friend , manager, my nephew and myself.

Sicarah: Absolutely I love it. I just want to ask you one quick fun question?

Mariah Lynn: I know you kind of choked me up a little bit girl.....

Sicarah: I know. I'm sorry let me put a little bit of fun back in there. If you could act with any male actor who would be your dream male actor?? Your dream male boyfriend?

Mariah Lynn: Actor? It would be of course Quincy. I mean; who wouldn't? Shout out to all three of Diddy's sons.They are all very handsome. If I had to choose one it would be Quincy , actor wise. If it was music I would go with Justin or maybe King Combs. I'm not sure which one but I'll take them all bring them all.

Sicarah: Right okay. Last but not least what's next for Mariah Lynn?

"I'm still here fighting."

Mariah Lynn: There is a bigger picture for Mariah Lynn. When I say a bigger picture I say I see artist like Cardi B. Excelling beyond expectations breaking barriers and setting records. I see other people doing the same thing. As far as like you know I see the Kash dolls and stuff like that I'm really excited about . I feel a lot of people tend to ask me this question. The following question is always where do you see yourself in five years ? where do you see yourself in the future? I'm like honestly what I really want to say is I don't know and that's because I trust my journey now. I used to get very frustrated with seeing people, not frustrated seeing them further themselves but more or less seeing myself being quick sand . It's like you see these people doing so great and I'm working so hard everyday. That's it's like why I am not where people think I should be? Or where I would want to be? It's because like I said there's a bigger picture. God has been preparing me for something bigger than what I could even imagine. I firmly believe that. That's why I say that this year is welcoming everybody including you to the evolution of Mariah Lynn.

Sicarah: I can't wait you guys heard it here first.

"Overall, you have to push through; no matter what."

COVER STORY

"NOT GET LOST IN THE SAUCE . LOSING YOUR MORALS AND YOU KNOW "BOW DOWN" IN CERTAIN SITUATIONS.

— **MARIAH LYNN**

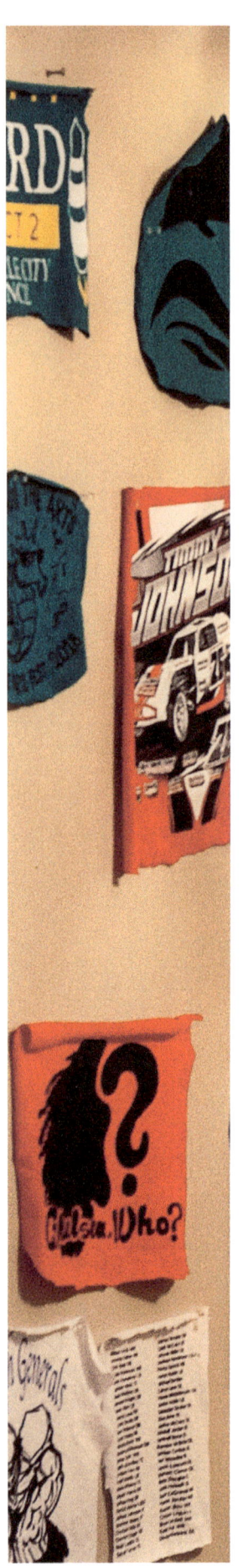

WELCOME TO
SOUTHERN GENTS PRINTING!

Southern Gents Printing is a Screen Printing shop located in the Huntsville, Alabama. SGP is offering a variety of custom printing and designing services. They specialize in printing soft hand, discharge, and water based inks on different promotional items. These items include but are not limited to t-shirts, yard signs, banners, hats, pens, table clothes, and bags. They offer quick, reliable, and friendly service where no job is too big or too small. For a pricing, submit your inquiries to sales@southerngentsprinting.com and keep an eye on your email for your custom quote to arrive. Our standard turnaround time is 10 business days, which allows our owner to personally oversee each project they take on.

"Thank you for your consideration and support. We look forward to printing for you! "

Fashion Gxd Magazine : How did the idea for your business come about
SGPC: My father started a print shop in his college dorm. He printed for his college in Mississippi and help many people start fashion lines in his area. He was inspired to help his community any way he could. Taking his entrepreneur blood and his care for his community I wanted to do the same in my community.

Fashion Gxd Magazine : How do you find people to bring into your organization that truly care about the organization the way you do?
SGPC:This is probably one of the hardest things. We go through a two hour interview process. For example we have 2 graphic/designers that are on staff. There minds has to be mentally ready for a when a customer comes in wanting to start a new clothing line. The customer trust us to give them the best design possible. This is something that most of the world will see so they have to be careful on how/what they design. Finding people that truly care about the art of clothing is hard. So we sometimes go out and find fashion designers that are starting out and they are trying to start a clothing line etc and say hey how about you come work for us and we will help you print your brand and get your clothing line going. Those are some of the people that have passion to the art. At Southern Gents Printing our motto for our printers and other crew members is (If you won't wear, it doesn't leave this warehouse). We love our employees they take pride in what comes from our shop. You have to take your time when finding someone to be on your team.

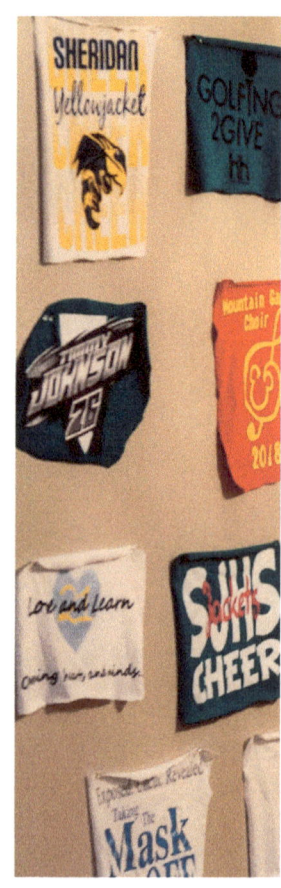

Fashion Gxd Magazine : What three pieces of advice would you give to other children who want to become entrepreneurs?
SGPC: 1) Follow your dreams - Remember where you came from and how you got started - Think outside the box

Fashion Gxd Magazine :What would you say are the top three skills needed to be a successful entrepreneur ?
SGPC: Management, Patience and Knowledge.

Fashion Gxd Magazine :What have been some of your failures, and what have you learned from them?
SGPC: My major failure was when I first started. I thought I knew how to run a business, so I didn't take advice from my father that was doing $500,000 a year. I thought his way was to slow and didn't make sense. Some of that was true but what I needed to know was the ins and outs of the business and how to be profitable. How to to run a business as a black male. My father let me fail i hit negative each month and sales, customers were angry my name pretty much was drugged through the mud.

IF WE WON'T WEAR IT, IT DOESN'T LEAVE OUT WAREHOUSE

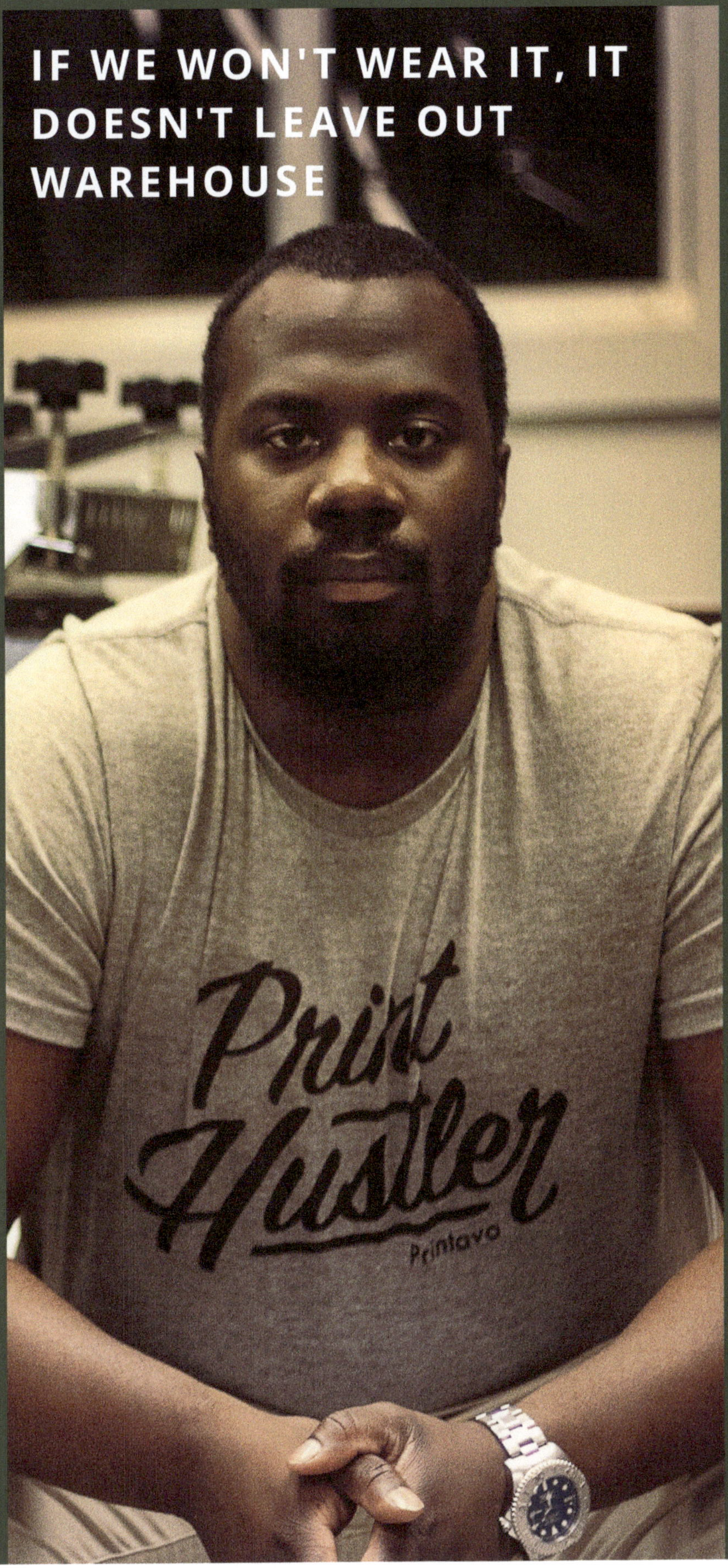

WWW.SOUTHERNGENTSPRINTING.COM
INSTAGRAM - @SOUTHERNGENTSPRINTING
FACEBOOK - SOUTHERN GENTS PRINTING LLC
EMAIL - SALES@SOUTHERNGENTSPRINTING.COM

Not know what to do I had to bite the bullet and ask for guidance. After failing I learned Big time that there are people out there that always knows more than you. You have to set your ego to the side and listen. I know besides my father have other mentors that I go to. I went from negative to $20,000 a month in sales. And now I handle million dollar contracts.

Fashion Gxd Magazine : How many hours do you work a day on average?
SGPC:13-14 hours a day. Success doesn't come overnight you have to work at it. Be hungry stay hunger. My thought process is that if you don't work at what you want/love and if you give up there is someone waiting to take what you have built and gave up on.

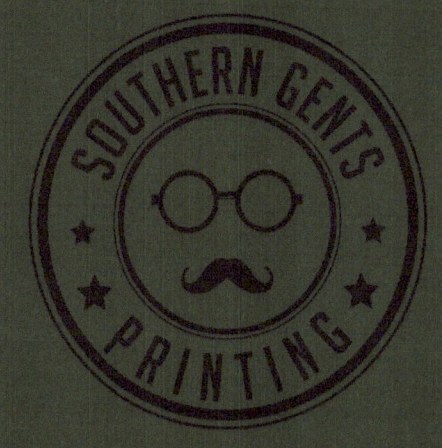

ENTREPENUERS 101

Thingaholic

STORY BY : SAMANTHA CEE

Tarren Tate Founder, Thingaholic has crossed 4000 units sold and climbing. The dynamic husband and wife duo has moved production for their most popular products to the United States and deliver your orders faster and more reliably. Thingaholic consists of photographic prints and products; (totes, shower curtains, duvet covers, phone/iPad covers, rugs, pillow covers, and so on) are custom-made in partnership with an outside company. Their products are all custom made to order. This means you choose exactly what you want to purchase and we produce it. We at Fashion Gxd Magazine has an exclusive interview with the rising brand. Take a look at the exclusive interview below.

Fashion Gxd Magazine : How do you find people to bring into your organization that truly care about the organization the way you do?
Tarren (CEO): It was easy! We started with just my husband and I, and that was it! We're a small team, just me and him but we hire family to help when things get overwhelmingly busy.

Fashion Gxd Magazine : What three pieces of advice would you give to other children who want to become entrepreneurs?
Tarren (CEO : Don't be afraid to fail. Take risks. The world tells people that a 9 to 5 is the only way to succeed. That is NOT TRUE. If you have an idea, DO IT.

Fashion Gxd Magazine : If you had the chance to start your career over again, what would you do differently?
Tarren (CEO : We would definitely have started sooner! Unfortunately, we waited for a while before we got the courage to jump.

Fashion Gxd Magazine : What would you say are the top three skills needed to be a successful entrepreneur ?

Tarren (CEO : Organization, grit (it gets hard sometimes!), and being self-driven. You are your own boss, push yourself!

Fashion Gxd Magazine : What have been some of your failures, and what have you learned from them?
Tarren (CEO : Lack of organization at the beginning. When we started we thought very small. We thought "oh, we'll sell something here or there, but it would be great if it blew up!". Well, it took off and we weren't prepared for the volume, and we learned very quickly that we needed to be able to scale up with demand smoothly. So we had to build platforms and use API to get things automated with our manufacturing facilities.

Fashion Gxd Magazine : How many hours do you work a day on average?
Tarren (CEO : Roughly about 12 hours. The thing about owning your own business and it being the way you eat is that you always have to hustle and be on to the next thing.

Fashion Gxd Magazine :Describe/outline your typical day?
Tarren (CEO : Mornings we'll have breakfast with the family and then we'll start work day planning either some new designs, ad and branding strategy or putting out a fire. After the morning brain dump, Brian will set about the task of designing and launching the product while I focus on dealing with the customers and manufacturing facilities to keep things running smoothly. Throughout the day things come up and we deal with them together as well.

Fashion Gxd Magazine : How has being an entrepreneur affected your family life?
Tarren (CEO : It's hard trying to balance everything and getting used to working again after Tarren has been a stay at home mom for 14 years. We also homeschool, but fortunately our kids are old enough to handle a majority of that on their own with the curriculum we use which is DVD based. Some things definitely get pushed to the weekends more than they did before. LOL, but the really nice thing is we can take breaks whenever we decide! Sometimes a trip to the park is the perfect getaway from emails and spreadsheets.

Fashion Gxd Magazine :What motivates you?
Tarren (CEO : Knowing that we're able to be self sufficient. Making our own money, being our own boss. The fact that this is even possible is exciting to us and I want to see how far we can take this!

Fashion Gxd Magazine : How do you generate new ideas?
Tarren (CEO : Several different ways! You have to keep your eye on what's out there. There's lots of ideas out there on social networks and just seeing what other people are doing and wearing. Then there are buyers that we have that always come back to buy more of what we have and they also give ideas for what we should put out next.

Fashion Gxd Magazine : What sacrifices have you had to make to be a successful entrepreneur?
Tarren (CEO : Time is a big one for us there. There used to be a lot of time for things like Netflix or TV, but those hours are filled now doing something for the business or the family. Fortunately, we love what we do!

Fashion Gxd Magazine : Where you see yourself and your business in 10 years? 20 years?
Tarren (CEO : The 10 year plan is to still be growing, but not only that but helping others grow! Early on when we started doing this we started getting messages from other people who saw us doing this and wondered how THEY could start a business, or how they could grow. People who already knew they wanted something different, but just didn't know how to get there. So we want to be doing a lot of supporting other entrepreneurs in that way as well!

PURCHASE BOOK:

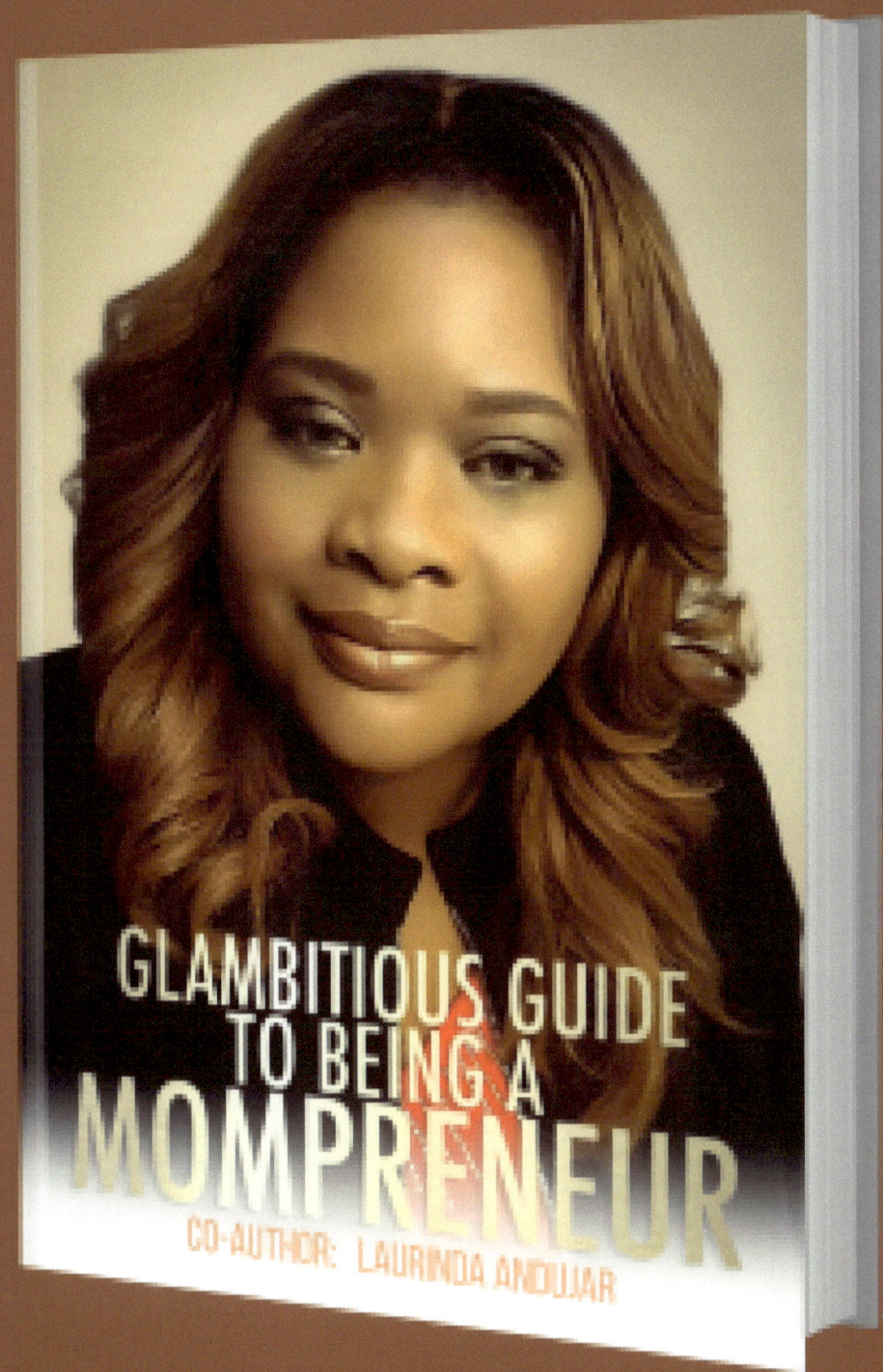

LAURINDA ANDUJAR

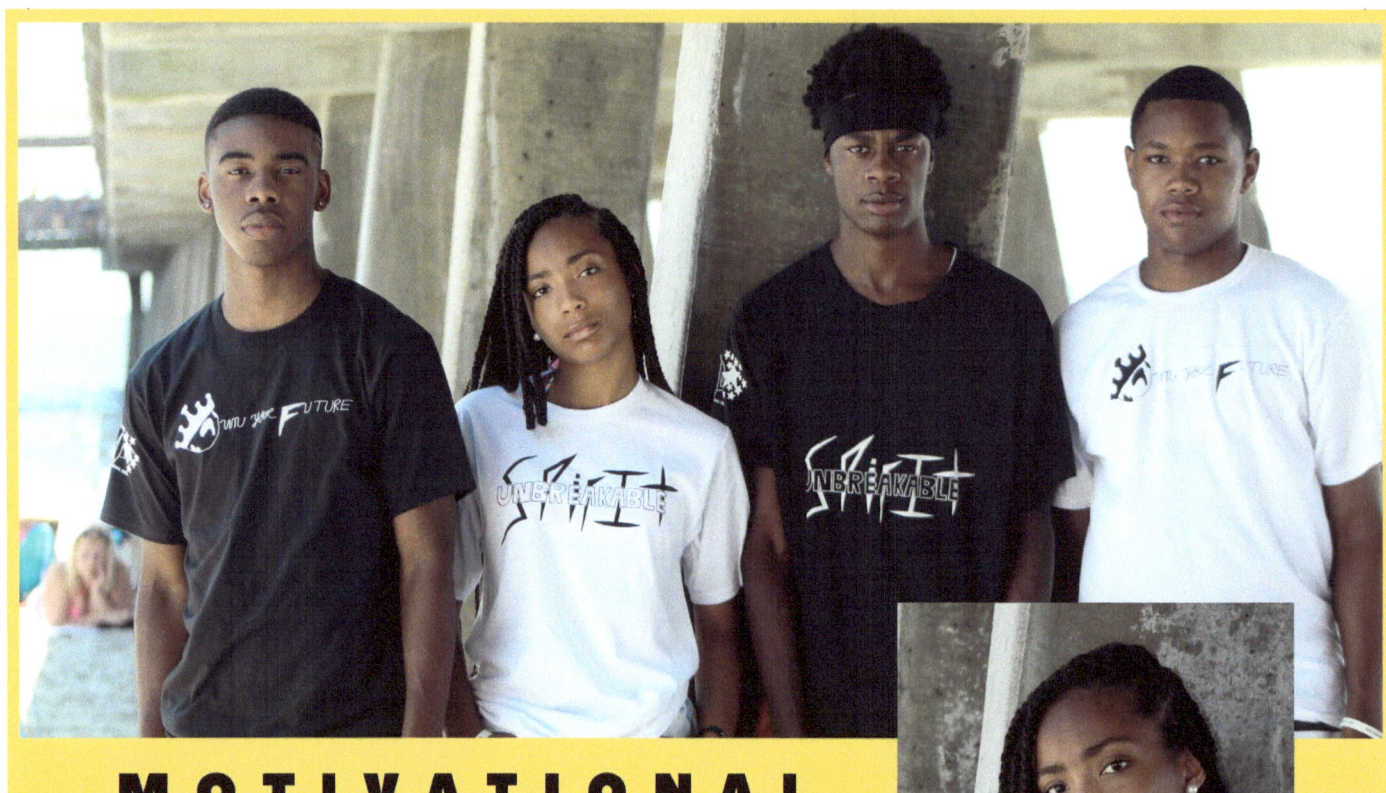

MOTIVATIONAL DESIGN

MOTIVATIONAL DESIGN IS A CLOTHING BRAND THAT PROMOTES SELF-MOTIVATION AND CONFIDENCE NOT AS A LIFESTYLE CHOICE BUT AS A MINDSET ONE CAN BUILD THEMSELVES TO ACHIEVE. TAKE A LOOK AT OUR EXCLUSIVE INTERVIEW WITH THE RISING BRAND.

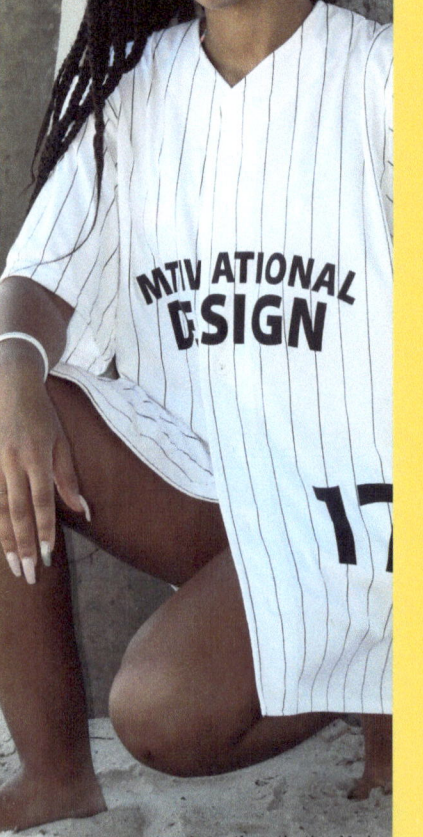

Fashion Gxd Magazine : How did the idea for your business come about?
Motivational Design: So the initial idea originally came from Me (Tramara) I felt as though there were not too many brands out there promoting motivation and confidence in people so I came up with some motivational phrases but I needed a creative touch to allow them to come to life. That is where my co-founder, Jerome comes in, with his artistic and creative mind and my logistical business mindset we came together and that is how Motivational Design came about.

Fashion Gxd Magazine : How do you find people to bring into your organization that truly care about the organization the way you do?
Motivational Design: We don't really go to people to bring on board our brand they actually come to us. We will get responses asking to promote for our brand or to be a part of the next photoshoot. While we do have a few brand ambassadors that assist with helping to promote, many people have been reaching out to us to be apart of our brand.

Fashion Gxd Magazine : What three pieces of advice would you give to other children who want to become entrepreneurs?

Motivational Design: First and foremost, NEVER GIVE UP it may seem difficult in the beginning stages, but it takes a lot of time and effort to create a successful business. Second, stay organized make sure you have everything that has to do with your business in order and not all over the place. Have everything in a clean space where everything is easy to find. Trust us, it will make your life much less complicated. Lastly, make sure your business venture is something you are passionate about. It will drive your MOTIVATION to want to be successful and continue to put 100% effort in your work.

FFashion Gxd Magazine :If you had the chance to start your career over again, what would you do differently?
Motivational Design: If we were to start over again we would have saved more money for our business. It is important to have enough funds to invest into your business as well as keeping it going because you may not make a huge profit right away.

Fashion Gxd Magazine :What would you say are the top three skills needed to be a successful entrepreneur ?
Motivational Design: The top three skills an entrepreneur should have is to stay focused, prioritize your time efficiently, and always be consistent.

Fashion Gxd Magazine :What have been some of your failures, and what have you learned from them?
Motivational Design: One of our main failures is not pricing our products correctly. We didn't realize how much went into figuring out our prices so, when we actually sat down to price how much it cost to make one product we realized we were overcharging for products and it was a turn off for some of our customers. Once we realized our mistake we changed the prices accordingly and it's made our customers very happy.

Fashion Gxd Magazine : How many hours do you work a day on average?
Motivational Design: So we both have side jobs on top of working on Motivational Design because we aren't making enough profit as of yet to be fully self employed however, on average we sit down and spend at least 2-5 hours a day working on things that need to be done such as discussing emails sent to us, fulfilling orders, news ways to promote as well as talking about events to sell our products at.s well as talking about events to sell our products at.

www.themotivationaldesign.com
motivation.is.my.design@gmail.com
Facebook: Motivational Design
Instagram: motivation.is.my.design
Twitter: MD_lifestylee

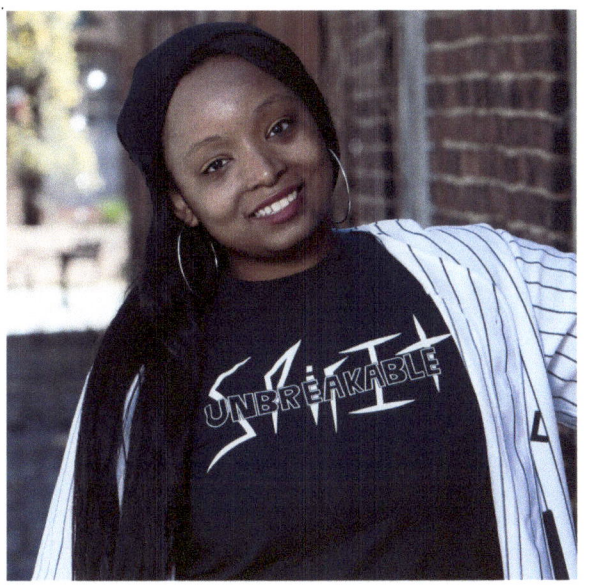

"STAY FOCUSED, PRIORITIZE YOUR TIME EFFICIENTLY, AND ALWAYS BE CONSISTENT"

FASHION GXD MAGAZINE : DESCRIBE/OUTLINE YOUR TYPICAL DAY?
MOTIVATIONAL DESIGN: WELL FIRST WE CHECK TO SEE IF WE HAVE ANY ORDERS TO FULFILL. WE CHECK TO SEE IF ANY EMAILS NEED TO BE RESPONDED TO AS FAR AS BUSINESS IS CONCERNED, THEN WE TALK ABOUT NEW WAYS TO MARKET OUR BRAND AND WE ARE PLANNING EVENTS SUCH AS PHOTOSHOOTS OR BOOTHS TO SELL AT.
FASHION GXD MAGAZINE : HOW HAS BEING AN ENTREPRENEUR AFFECTED YOUR FAMILY LIFE?

Motivational Design: It hasn't really affected our life too much although in the beginning some of our family members weren't completely on board with our ideas at first now they are very supportive wearing our products and telling people about our brand.

Fashion Gxd Magazine :What motivates you?
Motivational Design: Of course, our customers and supporters motivate us because they buy the products and give us feedback on our business which pushes us to do more. Even those that don't purchase our products but shout us out on social media and spreading the word of our brand we always appreciate them.

Fashion Gxd Magazine: How do you generate new ideas?
Motivational Design: We think about what our customers would like and research trending ideas that aren't exhibiting negativity and put our MD touch to the idea making it in line with what our brand stands for. Some ideas get turned into products but, not all our ideas make the cut as we strive to bring out better designs than the last.

Fashion Gxd Magazine : What sacrifices have you had to make to be a successful entrepreneur?
Motivational Design: The sacrifices we have made for our clothing brand is not being able to have a social life like most of the people in our age group. We are in our 20s and supposed to be living life and traveling the world however, we decided to put this part of our life on hold until we can build our brand well enough to where that may be possible at our own leisure.

Fashion Gxd Magazine : Where you see yourself and your business in 10 years? 20 years?
Motivational Design: In the next 10 years we see ourselves and our brand going places we never expected to go. We see our clothing brand everywhere in retail stores and we see ourselves planning speaking events for people to come listen of our journey towards being motivated and how they can be motivated as well. In 20 years we hope to not only have Motivational Design under our belt but multiple business ventures that all can function without our direct supervision. It seems like a long journey to get to that point or almost impossible however, we know how much time and effort we have to put into Motivational Design to make it to that milestone and make it possible.

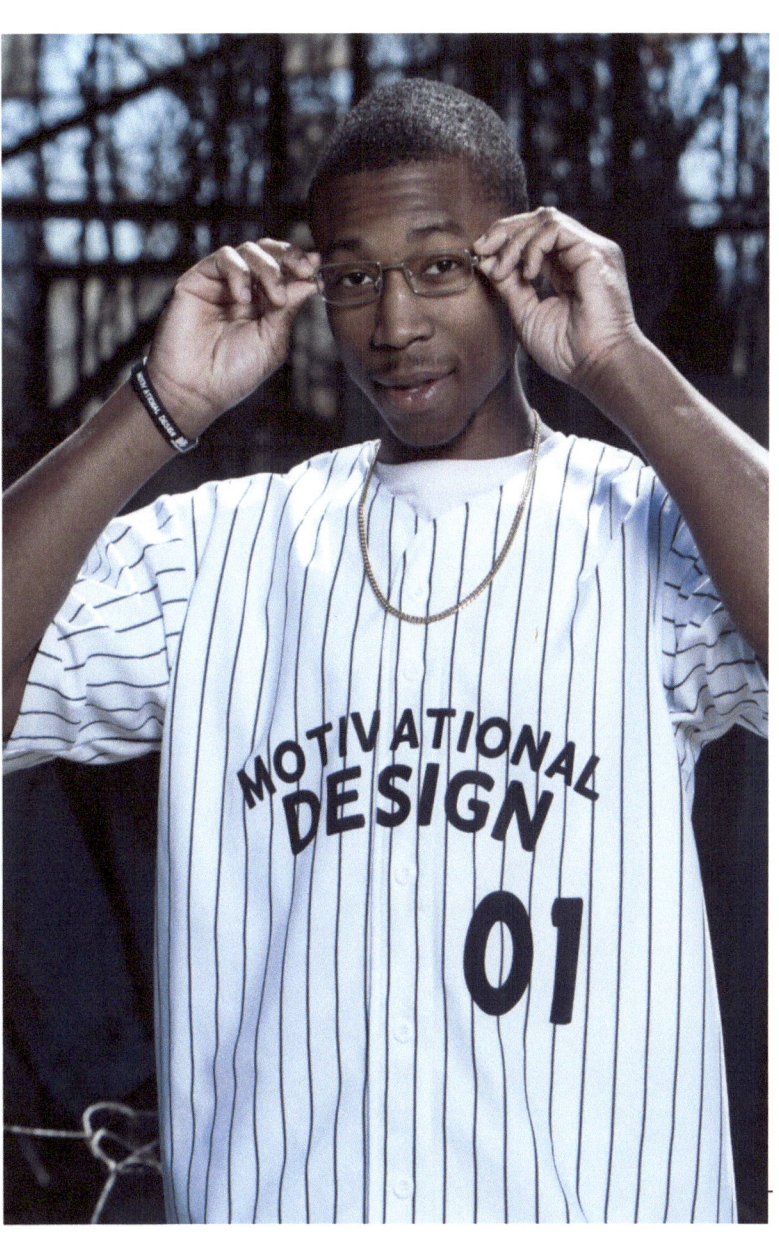

Jess Mi BOUTIQUE

At Jess Mi Boutique, we combine class and alluring looks into one to make the everyday woman feel not so everyday. We carry items such as matching sets, sporting wear, dresses, jumpsuits, swimsuits, and more. CEO, Jess Michelle, wanted to give women classy styles without compromising their sexy; not to mention super affordable.

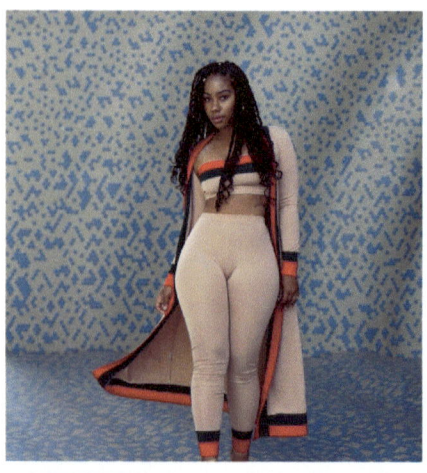
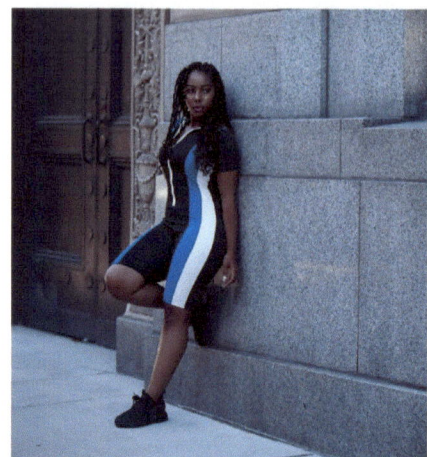
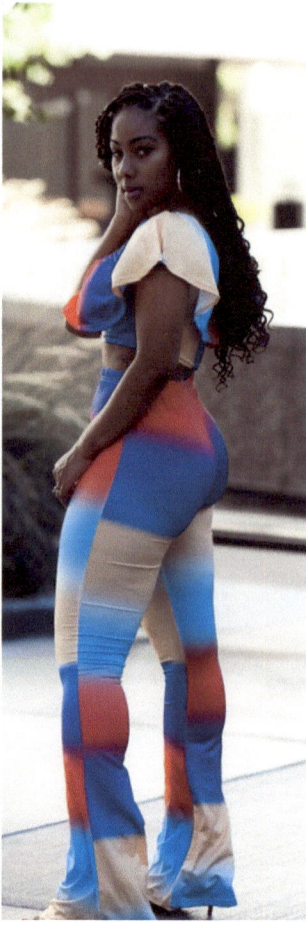
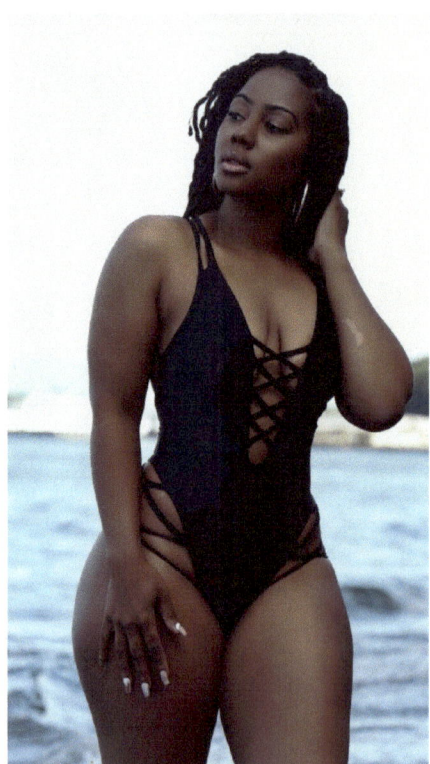
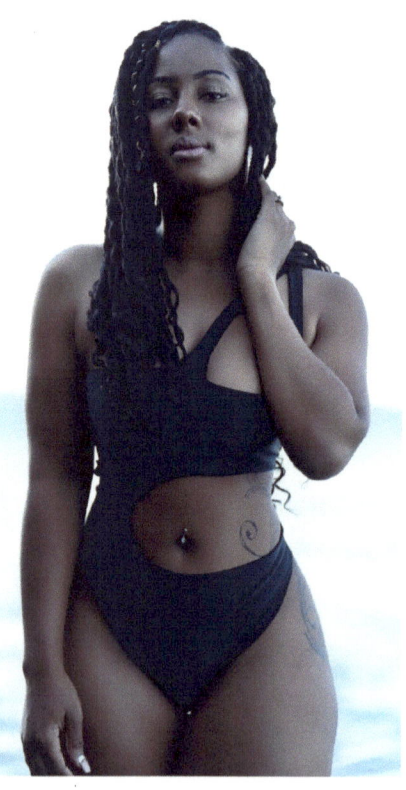

SOCIAL CONTACT

Jess Mi Boutique
Instagram: @jessmi_boutique
Facebook: Jess Mi Boutique (@jessmiboutique)
Website: JessMiBoutique.com

Jess Michelle (Owner/Model)
Instagram: @only1jessmichelle
Facebook: Jess Michelle (@only1jessmichelle)

Photographers
Tanisha Frazier
Instagram: @mcphotography/ @agirlwithvision

Christopher Munson
Instagram: @munson253

FASHION GXD MAGAZINE

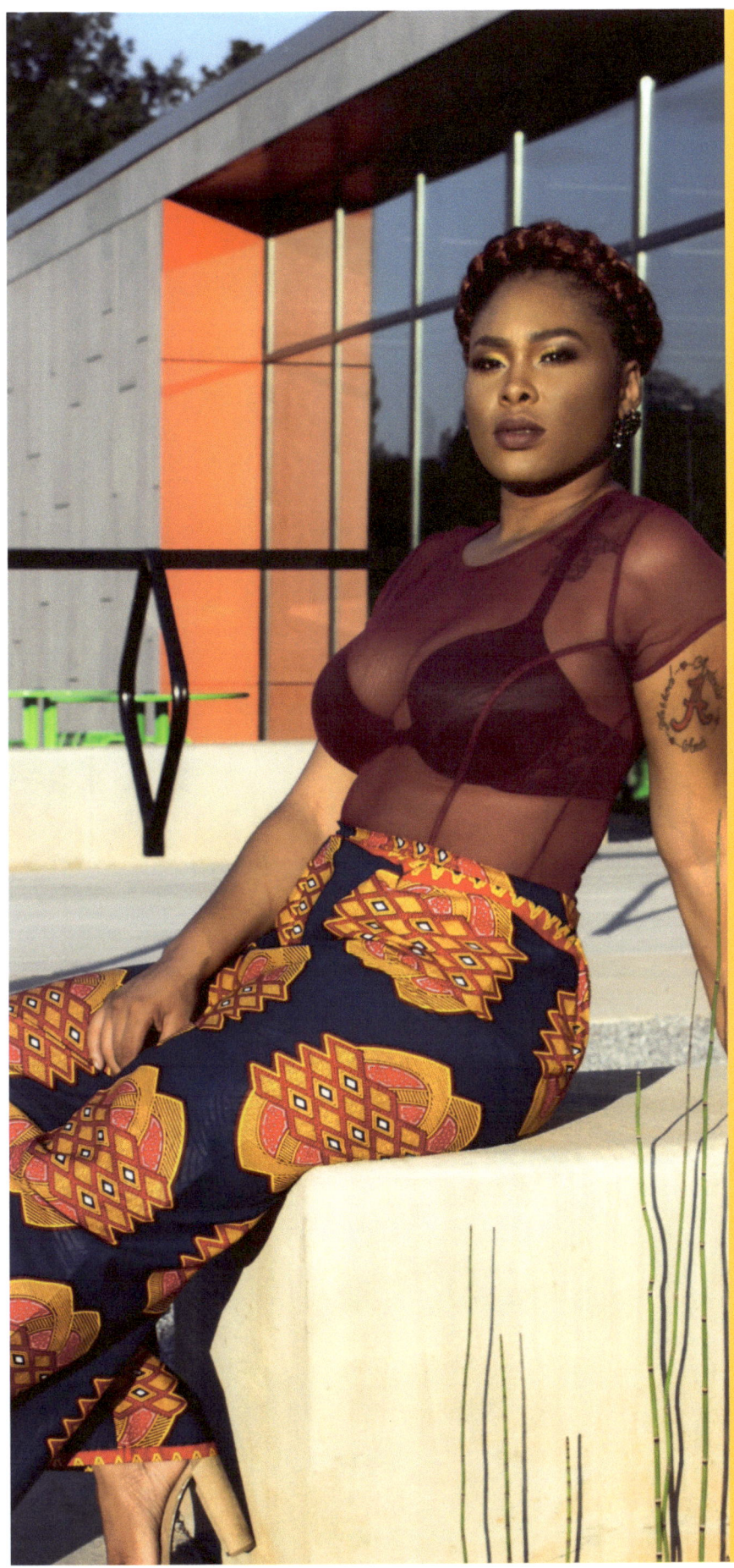

SERVE UP SUCCESS WITH ASYA DOMIQUE

HUETIFUL ELEVATION, AKA THE MELANATED FASHION HOUSE, IS A LUXURY FASHION BRAND THAT PROVIDES CUSTOM AND TAILOR MADE GARMENTS INSPIRED BY THE VARIOUS CULTURES OF MELANATED BEINGS. WE PROVIDE A COUTURE EXPERIENCE FOR OUR CLIENTS & THEY RECEIVE AN UPSCALE EXPERIENCE PROVIDED FOR US. BY US. TAKE A LOOK AT OUR EXCLUSIVE IFACTS ON SUCCES WE GAINED WITH THE RISING BRAND

FIVE SECRETS TO SUCCESS

1. Believe in Yourself
2. Stay Authentic in a world of constant changes
3. Learn from the Failures
4. Learn to Flow With the River, instead of Against Her
5. Never Forget Why You Started.

Facebook & Instagram :
BRAND@HuetifulElevation
PERSONAL @AsyaDomique

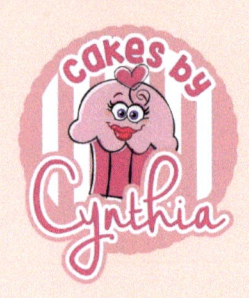

> Cakes by Cynthia is a dessert company providing custom cakes for all occasions wholesale distribution and Cupcake Truck

CYNTHIA KNOX

CLEAN TIPS

Social Media Accounts:
Instagram: cakes_by_cynthia
Facebook: cakesbycynthiaLLC
Twitter: cakesbycynthia2
Website: cakesbycynthia.net

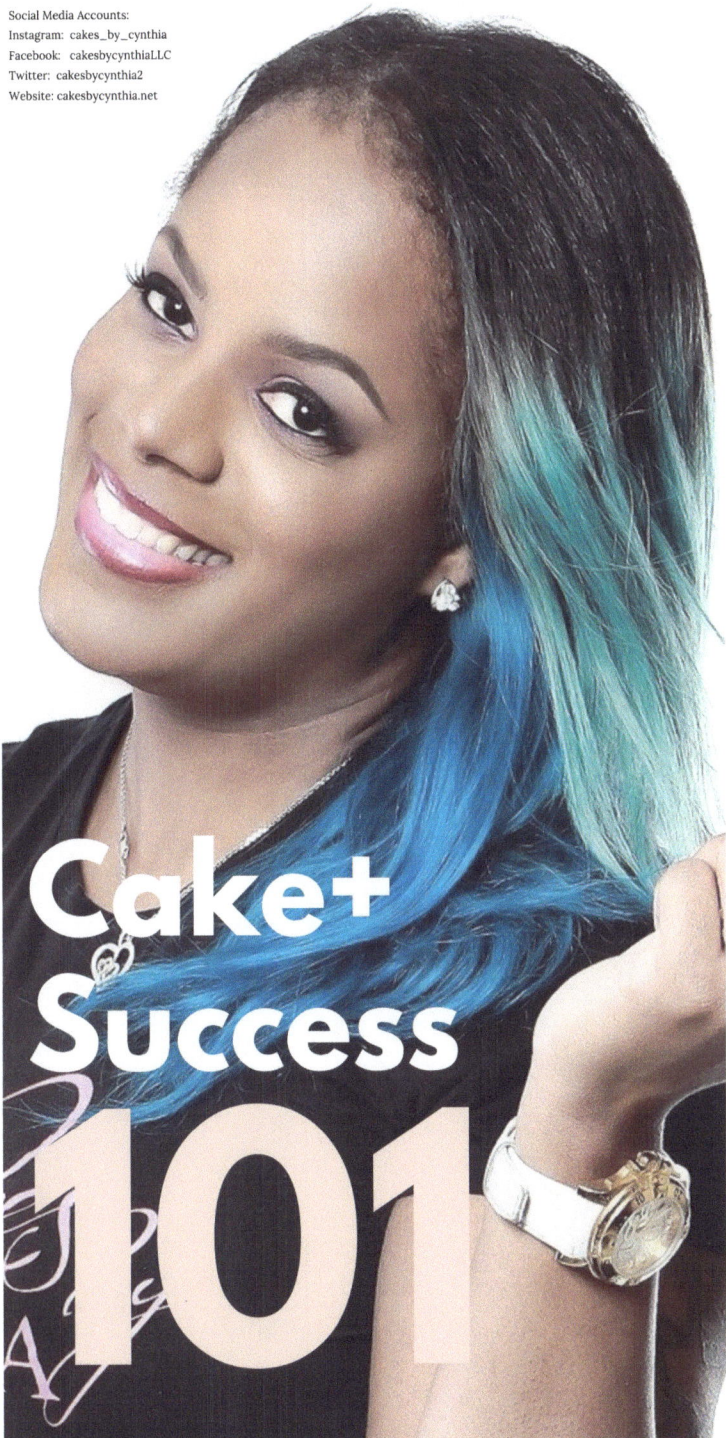

Cake+ Success 101

This month we sat down with the Queen of Cakes, Cynthia Knox. Cynthia is a successful CEO for Maryland. In 2005, Cakes by Cynthia was an official business. She went through many trails and tribulations to achieve the success she now has. It wasn't an easy "CAKE WALK", but she operated her business in three retail stores before moving into her current location in Arbutus, MD.

Cynthia has also appeared on national TV on The Cooking Channel "Cake Hunters", WETv "Wedding Cake Wars", Local News WBAL, FOX 45, FOX DC 5, Netflix "Sugar Rush", Magazine publications and often gives back to the community especially Baltimore City Public Schools with fundraisers and as a guest speaker sharing her story. Take a look at the five tips Cynthia gave us for her secrets to success.

FIVE TIPS FOR SUCCESS

1. Find your niche .... it may take several tries before you get it right...think of what kind of bakery you want to be... what do you wanna specialize in
2. Its ok to get stuck, just dont stay stuck!
3. Always remain consistent to your brand .... Packaging is key (well at least 1 of them..lol)
4. To achieve as much as you can for your growing business, make sure its in order... especially with credentials
5. Just use the initial business as the base business ... have several other entities under that umbrella ... expand your brand!

MATCH MADE IN FASHION HEAVEN

NYKWALE" is a clothing brand inspired by various beautiful African cultures. It is a brand that will make you feel bold and brave. Wearing NYKWALE is more than just wearing clothes... It's a lifestyle. To be seen, to be heard and to be understood.

WHAT EVEN?

NYKWALE is a brand that is inspired by the freedom and Artistry of millennial's of today. It is a brand that was created with intention to broaden the horizons of African culture. We use African prints more often but we will never evolve if we keep using them in the same ways. This brand shows character and innovation in a way that hasn't been done before. It is a mixture of Urban Street, Afrocentric, High fashion and just a hint of a sportswear which shouldn't make sense but it does in every way!

NYKWALE is in the works of becoming the next huge brand in the fashion industry and not just the African fashion industry but in the world. Because it's about time an Afrocentric brand takes high fashion by storm.

Live to be different. Be your best self and wear NYKWALE so they know it's real.

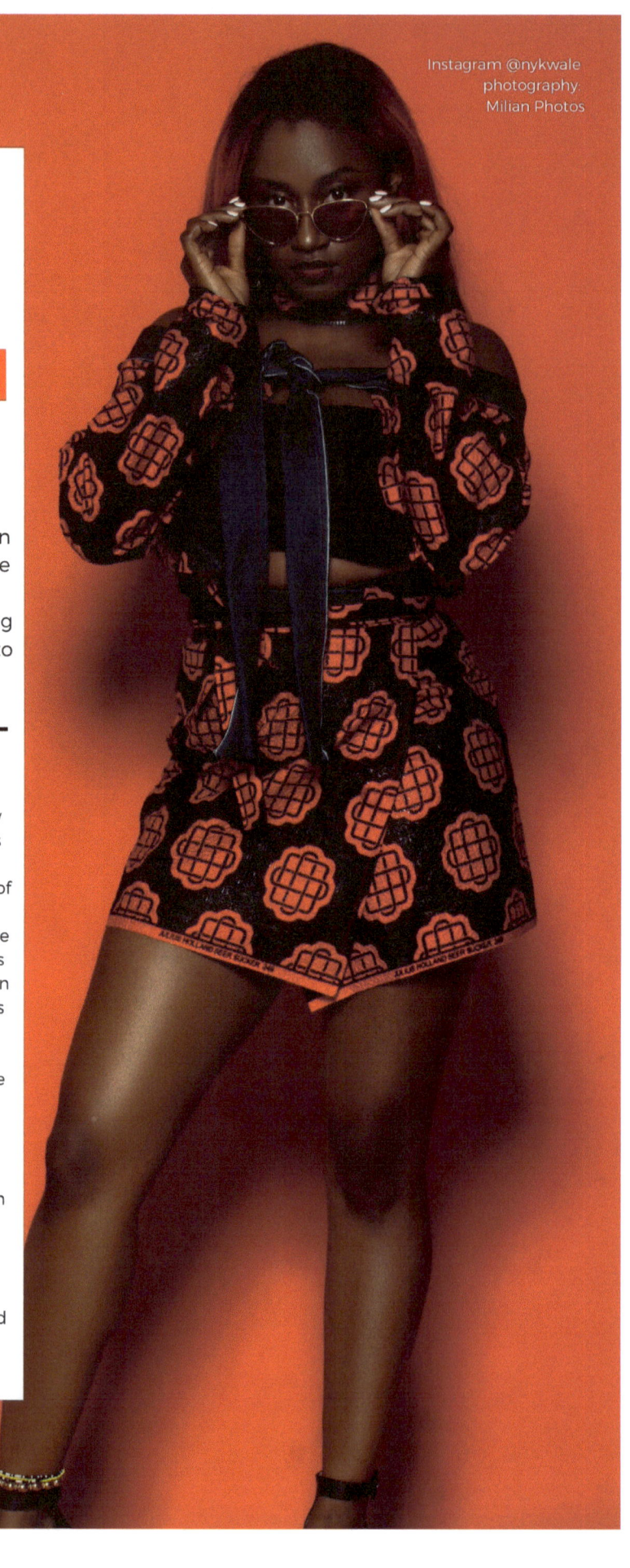

Instagram @nykwale
photography:
Milian Photos

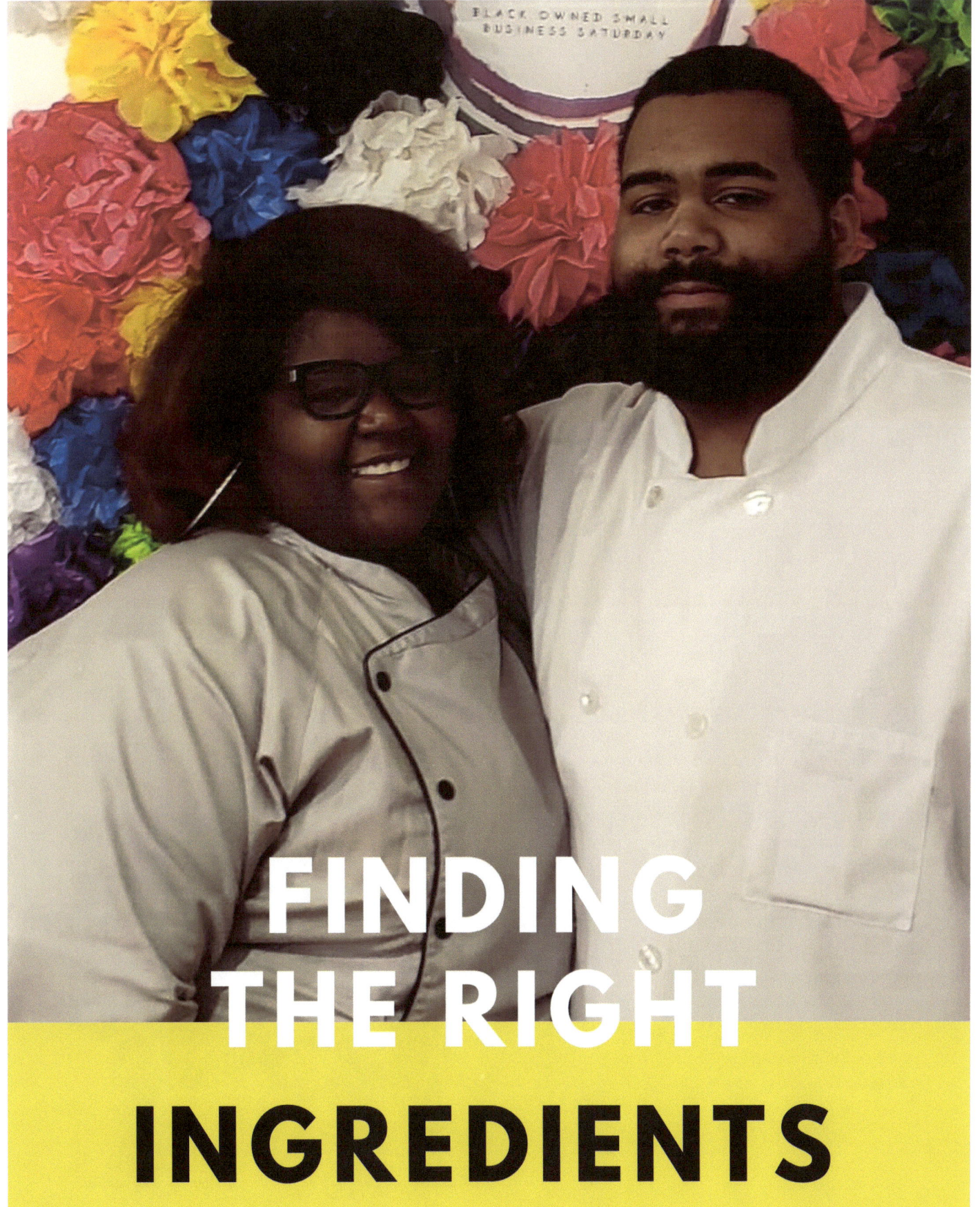

FINDING THE RIGHT INGREDIENTS

FEATURES

5 Tips to Becoming a Successful Entrepreneur in Your Industry

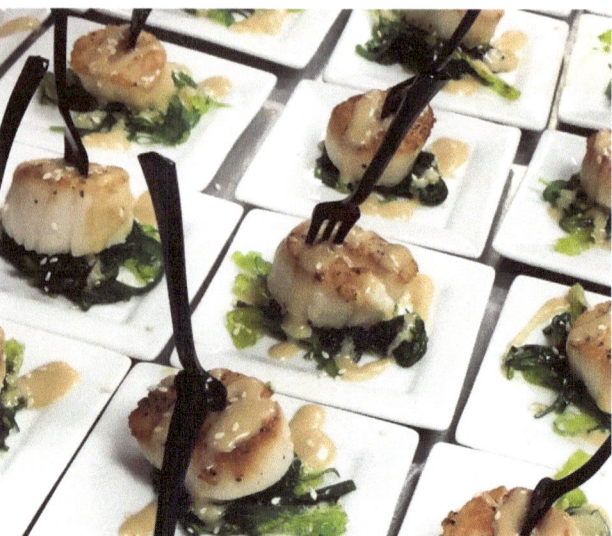

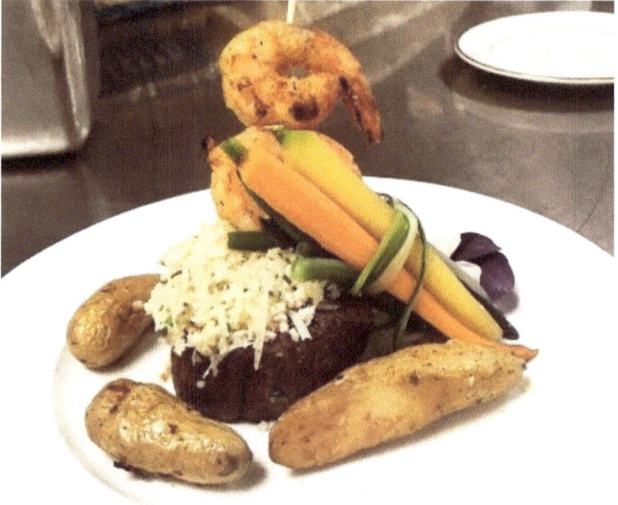

Based in New York, Serenity's Sweet & Savory Boutique is ran by couple Chef Na'Kia & Chef Jay. They specialize in custom cakes/sweet treats, Soul Food & Caribbean Cuisines, and catering for any occasion. At Serenity's Boutique they strive to produce the best quality product by using the freshest ingredients to create every homemade savory dish and every scratch-made sweet treat. Their mission is to give their clients an experience they'll never forget by inviting them into their kitchen and welcoming them as family! Take a look at the exclusive interview with Fashion Gxd Magazine.

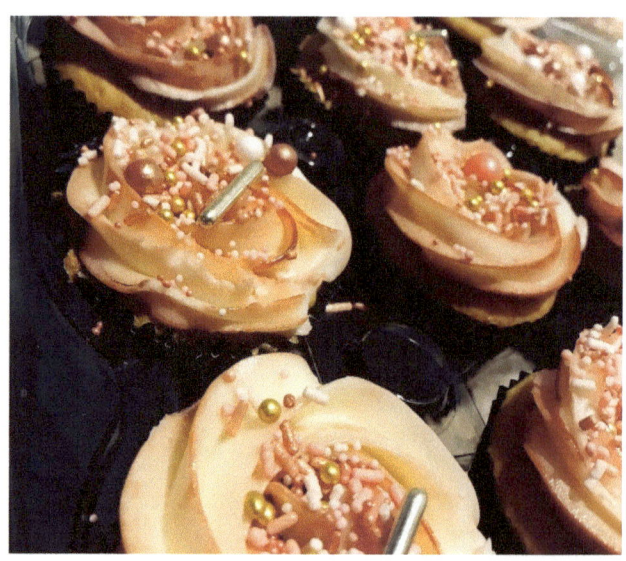

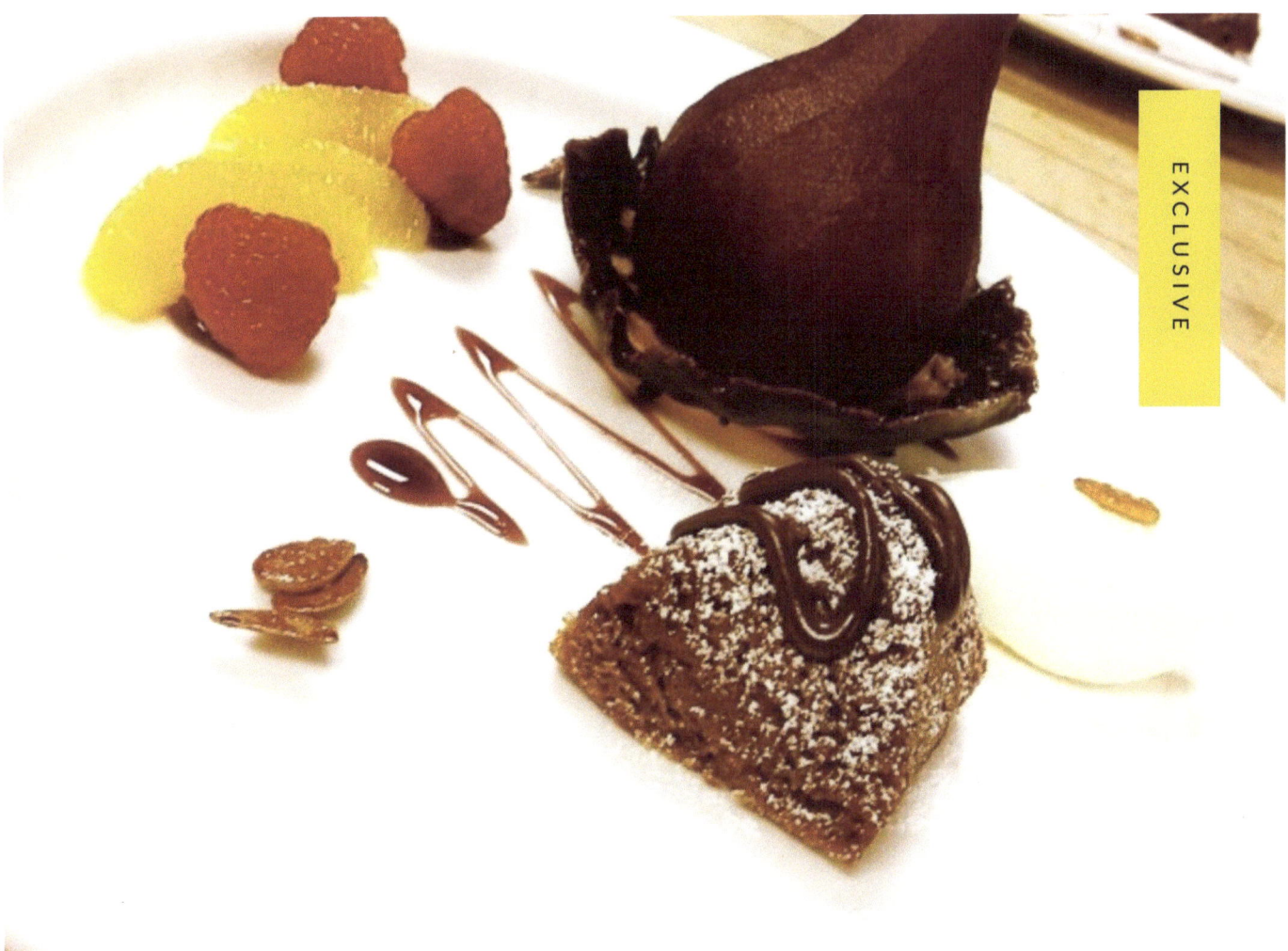

EXCLUSIVE

CHEF NA'KIA & CHEF JAY

Instagram- @SerenitysBoutique_
Facebook- SerenityBoutique12
www.SerenitysBoutiqueNYC.com

WRITTEN BY SAANTHA CEE

NETWORK & COLLABORATION

- Putting your self out there by networking and collaborating with other entrepreneurs. Attending business networking mixers, vendors events, and hosting events with other businesses are just a few example for you to help circulate your brand .

DON'T BE AFRAID TO ASK FOR HELP

-Often time small businesses start with just one person running the show. At first that maybe fine, but eventually business will pick up and you will find your self burnt out. Just because funds are not able to afford you to hire help doesn't mean you can't get any.

. STAY ACTIVE ON SOCIAL MEDIA

- Social media plays a big role in how businesses operate and gather a following of customers. Different media platforms have "hotspot" times when users are most likely to scroll through the apps, which helps business owners know who to target their products towards. Staying active on social media increases your presence and allows for your content to capture a broader audience. Using relevant hashtags helps draw in the audience that is looking for posts like yours and similar to yours. Be sure to use hashtags related to your business and always use the hashtags that have a greater number of posts. This will help widen your presence on social media.

. KNOWING WHAT YOUR CLIENT'S WANTS AND NEEDS ARE

-Knowing your clientele is a huge factor into being a successful entrepreneur. Knowing what your clients wants needs are helps you to determine what products and services you are going to offer. Post surveys on your social media account to help with determining your clientele's likes and dislikes.

. TURN YOUR PASSION INTO PROFIT

Doing what you love and offering it in your business is the best way to make sure that you will continue stay afloat in the big sea of entrepreneurs. Many entrepreneurs often fail by not going into business doing something that there are passionate about. "Do what you love, and you'll never work another day in your life."

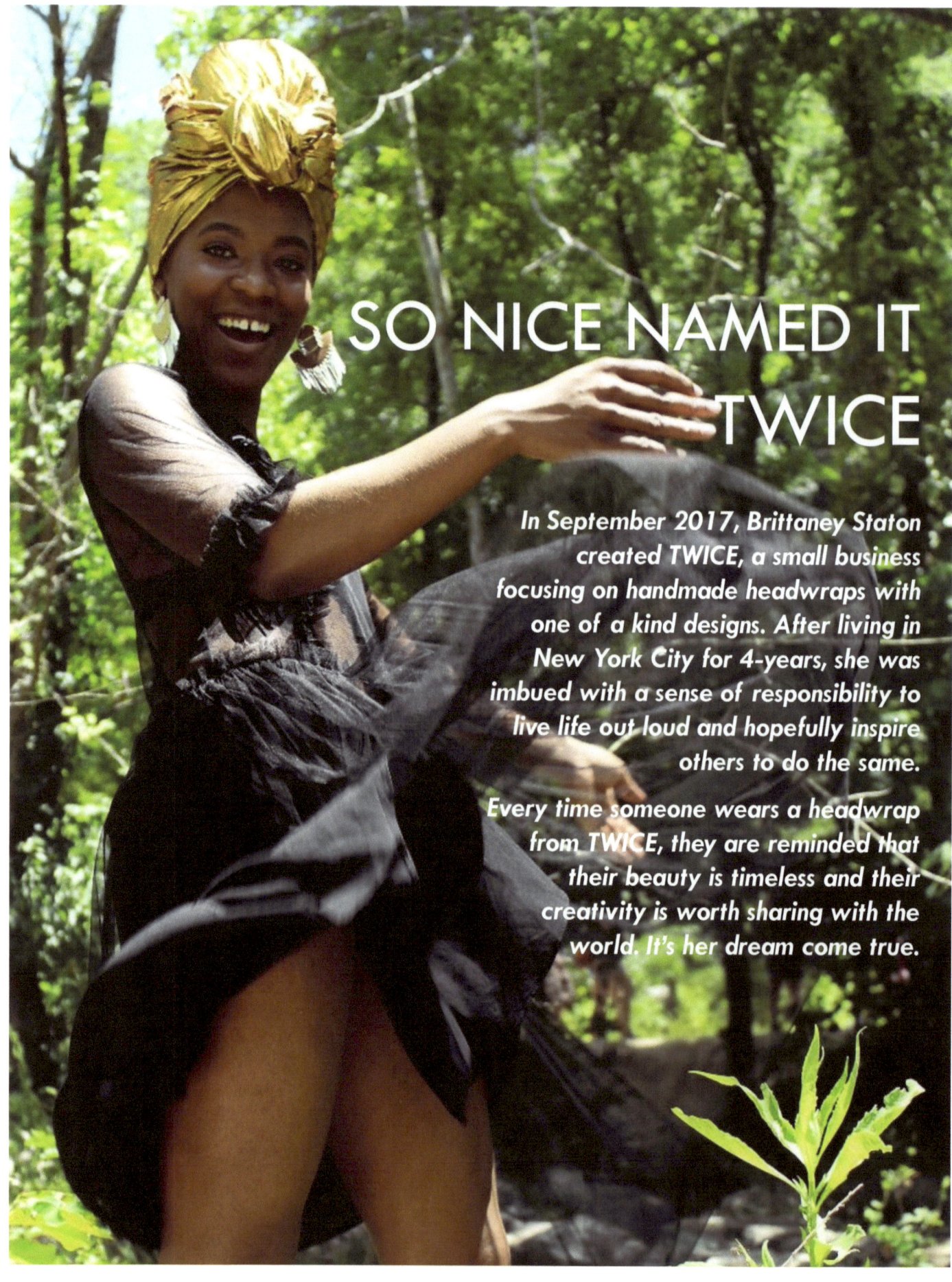

SO NICE NAMED IT TWICE

In September 2017, Brittaney Staton created TWICE, a small business focusing on handmade headwraps with one of a kind designs. After living in New York City for 4-years, she was imbued with a sense of responsibility to live life out loud and hopefully inspire others to do the same.

Every time someone wears a headwrap from TWICE, they are reminded that their beauty is timeless and their creativity is worth sharing with the world. It's her dream come true.

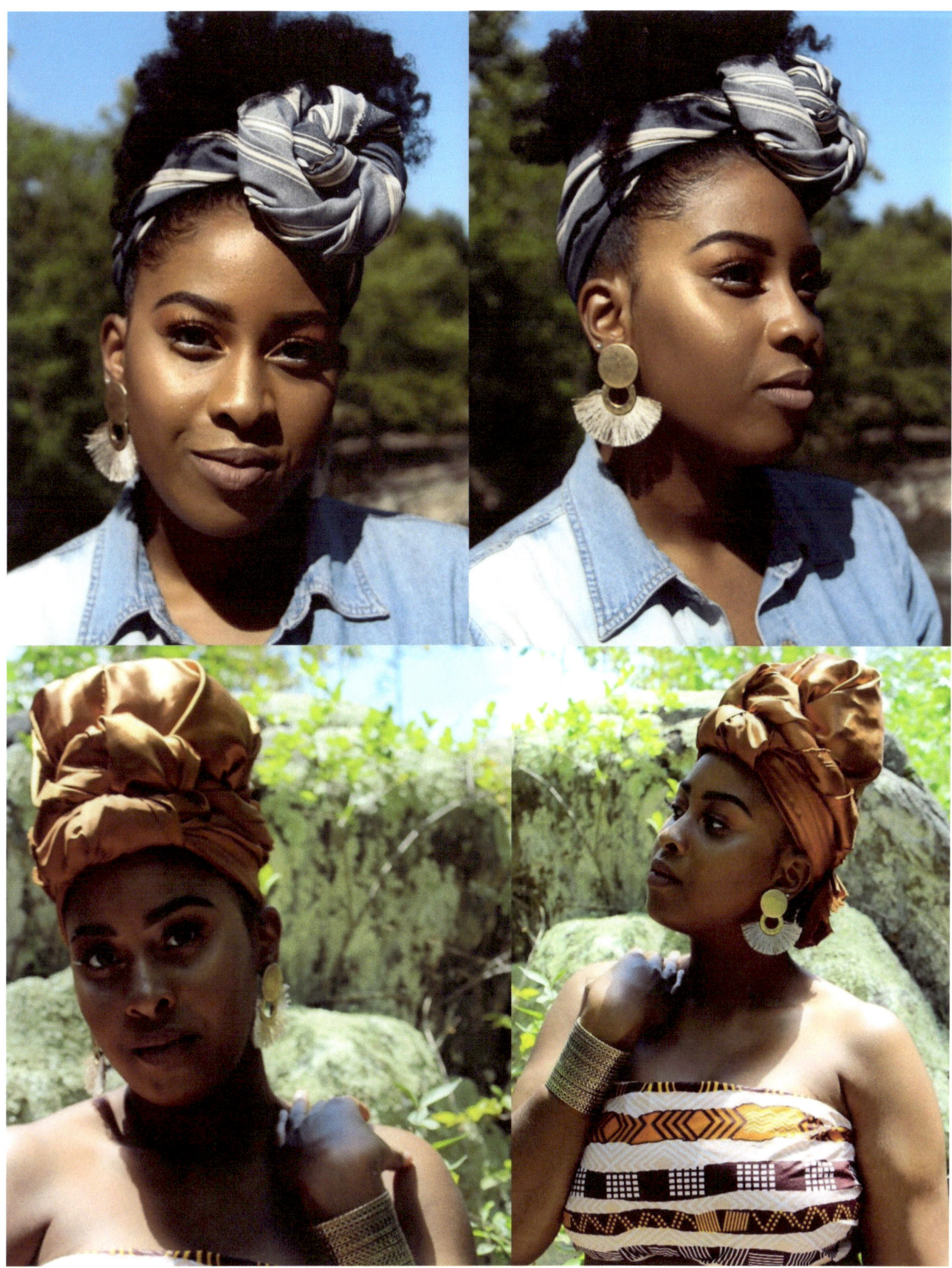

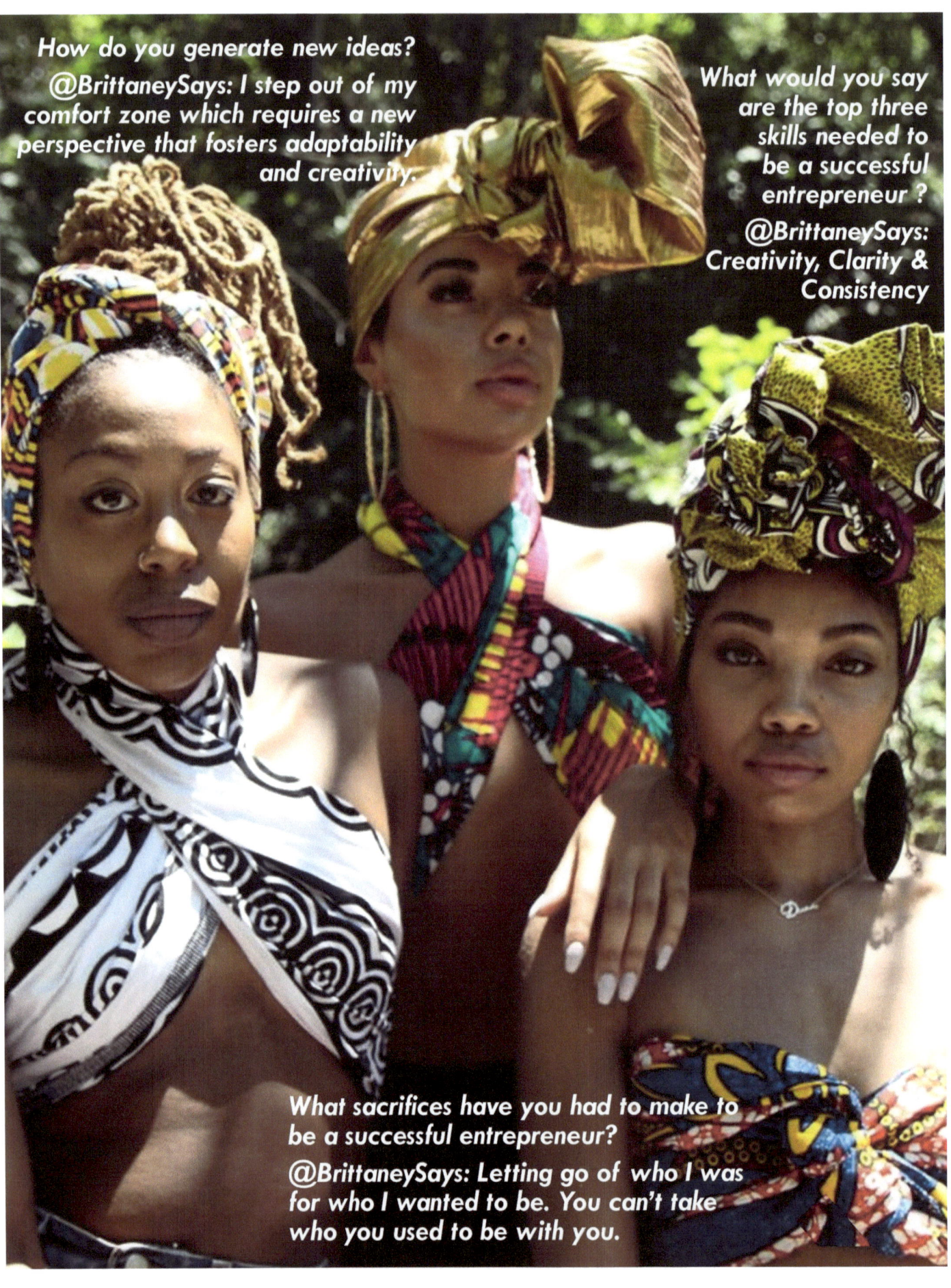

How do you generate new ideas?
@BrittaneySays: I step out of my comfort zone which requires a new perspective that fosters adaptability and creativity.

What would you say are the top three skills needed to be a successful entrepreneur?
@BrittaneySays: Creativity, Clarity & Consistency

What sacrifices have you had to make to be a successful entrepreneur?
@BrittaneySays: Letting go of who I was for who I wanted to be. You can't take who you used to be with you.

september 2018

Staff Directory.

Fashion Gxd Magazine

issue 02

Editor-in-chief Pilar Scratch

Publicist	**Terrell Everett**
Lead Makeup Artist	**Nydia Figueroa**
Assistant MUA	**Kelly Cortland**
Photogrpahy Director	**Notorious Photos**
Cover Fashion Designer	**Phoniex Elite**
Second Fashion Designer	**Marquise Foster**
Third Fashion Designer	**Kree Kreations**
Lead Wardrobe Stylist	**Andre Vonboozier**
Assistant Wardrobe Stylist	**Moon Iciana**
Accessories	**Velvz Monroe**
Studios	**Prince Street Studios**
Lashes	**Red Luxe Collection**
Cover Story	**SICARAH**

Fashion Gxd Magazine is published independently by CS Media Group.
2 Prince Street, Brooklyn, NY 11552 | @FashionGxdMAgazine

www.fashiongxxd.com

FASHION GXD MAGAZINE